grills

UNDER THE GRILL • GRILL PAN • BARBECUE

THE AUSTRALIAN
Women's Weekly

contents

We loved the challenge of taking the very traditional and deeply embedded custom of barbecue or grill cooking and coming up with a smorgasbord of clever and inspiring recipes. We learned from the experience, too: there's no need to spend hours on preparation or cleaning up after you've eaten, thanks to using so few mixing bowls, saucepans and the like. Great, easy meals and less washing up – it doesn't get much better than that.

Pamela Clark

Food Director

grist for the grill

Cooking can be as much fun as eating with a little pre-planning

Grilling can become more than just a cooking method for the health conscious; it can virtually be a lifestyle choice. Little added fat is called for in most grilling recipes, and much of the fat contained in the ingredients drains away during the cooking process. Plus, the high heat source helps capture flavour and moisture, both of which enhance the finished food's taste. Successful grilling is contingent on three main techniques: having the heat source at its optimum level for the food before you start cooking; organising all of a recipe's ingredients before you begin; and knowing how to identify when the food is done to your liking. It's a good idea to preheat the barbecue or grill pan to the highest level before you begin cooking to seal in flavourful juices. Prepare and set out all of the recipe's required ingredients and necessary tools while you're heating the grill. Testing for doneness is largely determined by appearance, feel and lots of practice. Grill-cooking will become second nature very quickly, and you'll constantly be surprised at the variety of ingredients that adapt so easily and deliciously to this enduring cooking method.

vegetables

And you thought the grill was the exclusive realm of the carnivore

felafel wraps

PREPARATION TIME 30 MINUTES (PLUS REFRIGERATION TIME) COOKING TIME 15 MINUTES SERVES 4

¾ cup (110g) frozen broad beans,
  thawed, peeled
420g can chickpeas, rinsed, drained
⅓ cup coarsely chopped fresh
  flat-leaf parsley
1 small red onion (100g),
  chopped coarsely
⅓ cup (50g) plain flour
2 teaspoons ground coriander
1 teaspoon ground cumin
1 egg
1 teaspoon bicarbonate of soda
4 large pitta breads (320g)
1 cup (260g) hummus
50g mesclun

MARINATED GRILLED EGGPLANT
6 baby eggplants (360g),
  sliced thinly lengthways
2 tablespoons olive oil
2 cloves garlic, crushed
1 tablespoon white wine vinegar
1 tablespoon finely chopped
  fresh flat-leaf parsley

1 Blend or process beans, chickpeas, parsley, onion, flour, spices, egg and soda until almost smooth. Shape rounded tablespoons of mixture into 16 felafel patties. Place on tray, cover; refrigerate 30 minutes.
2 Meanwhile, make marinated grilled eggplant.
3 Cook felafel on heated oiled flat plate until browned both sides. Spread pittas with hummus; top with mesclun, eggplant and felafel, roll to enclose filling.
MARINATED GRILLED EGGPLANT Cook eggplant on heated oiled flat plate until lightly browned both sides. Combine eggplant in medium bowl with remaining ingredients.
per serving 25.5g total fat (4.4g saturated fat); 2738kJ (655 cal); 74.2g carbohydrate; 24.3g protein; 17.1g fibre

POTATOES
ON THE SIDE

mediterranean smash

rosemary and garlic wedges

blue-cheese baked potatoes

potatoes byron

barbecued kumara slices

bacon and cheese potatoes

capsicum mash

onion and potato hash

mediterranean smash

PREPARATION TIME 15 MINUTES COOKING TIME 30 MINUTES SERVES 6

Preheat grill. Boil 1kg unpeeled baby new potatoes until tender; drain. Place on oven tray; grill until browned. Combine ⅓ cup olive oil, ¼ cup shredded fresh basil and 3 crushed garlic cloves in small saucepan; cook over low heat 15 minutes. Smash potatoes in large bowl with strained basil oil. Stir in ⅓ cup sliced seeded kalamata olives and ¼ cup shredded fresh basil.

per serving 12.4g total fat (1.7g saturated fat); 953kJ (228 cal); 23.3g carbohydrate; 4g protein; 3.2g fibre

rosemary and garlic wedges

PREPARATION TIME 10 MINUTES COOKING TIME 40 MINUTES SERVES 4

Preheat oven to moderately hot. Cut 1kg unpeeled kipfler potatoes into wedges. Combine in bowl with 6 chopped rosemary sprigs, 2 tablespoons olive oil and 2 crushed garlic cloves. Roast wedges on oven tray about 40 minutes or until tender.

per serving 9.4g total fat (1.3g saturated fat); 1066kJ (255 cal); 33.2g carbohydrate; 6.1g protein; 5.3g fibre

blue-cheese baked potatoes

PREPARATION TIME 10 MINUTES COOKING TIME 1 HOUR SERVES 4

Pierce 4 large unpeeled potatoes with fork; wrap in foil. Cook potatoes on barbecue, using indirect heat, about 1 hour. Grill 60g prosciutto until crisp. Cut cross in potatoes; squeeze with tongs to open. Divide combined ¾ cup sour cream and 50g crumbled blue cheese among potatoes, sprinkle with crumbled prosciutto.

per serving 24g total fat (15.3g saturated fat); 1877kJ (449 cal); 41g carbohydrate; 13.6g protein; 6g fibre

potatoes byron

PREPARATION TIME 10 MINUTES COOKING TIME 20 MINUTES SERVES 6

Oil six shallow 1-cup pie dishes. Boil 1kg potatoes until tender; drain. Preheat grill. Mash potato in large bowl with 300ml cream, 60g butter and 4 thinly sliced spring onions. Divide potato among dishes; sprinkle with ½ cup finely grated parmesan. Grill about 5 minutes or until browned.

per serving 32.3g total fat (21.2g saturated fat); 1764kJ (422 cal); 23.8g carbohydrate; 7.8g protein; 3.5g fibre

barbecued kumara slices

PREPARATION TIME 15 MINUTES COOKING TIME 25 MINUTES SERVES 6

Cut 2 large kumara into 1cm slices; boil until tender, drain. Cook kumara on heated oiled grill plate until browned; turn, brush with combined 1 crushed garlic clove, 2 tablespoons golden syrup, 2 teaspoons balsamic vinegar and ¼ teaspoon ground cinnamon.

per serving 0.2g total fat (0g saturated fat); 443kJ (106 cal); 23.3g carbohydrate; 2.2g protein; 2.1g fibre

bacon and cheese potatoes

PREPARATION TIME 20 MINUTES COOKING TIME 30 MINUTES SERVES 6

Boil 6 large potatoes until tender; drain. Cook 1 thinly sliced medium brown onion and 3 coarsely chopped bacon rashers in heated oiled frying pan until browned. Preheat grill. Cut and discard shallow slice from each potato. Scoop two-thirds of potato from each shell; place shells on baking-paper-lined oven tray. Discard half the potato flesh; combine remainder in bowl with bacon mixture, ⅓ cup sour cream and ⅓ cup grated cheddar. Spoon mixture into shells; top with 1 tablespoon coarsely grated cheddar. Grill until cheese browns. Sprinkle with 2 teaspoons finely chopped fresh chives.

per serving 11.2g total fat (6.4g saturated fat); 1275kJ (305 cal); 35g carbohydrate; 12.5g protein; 5.4g fibre

capsicum mash

PREPARATION TIME 15 MINUTES COOKING TIME 30 MINUTES SERVES 6

Quarter and roast 2 seeded large red capsicums; slice thinly. Boil 1kg potatoes until tender, drain; mash with ½ cup cream and 40g butter; stir in capsicum.

per serving 14.8g total fat (9.6g saturated fat); 1137kJ (272 cal); 26.6g carbohydrate; 6g protein; 3.8g fibre

onion and potato hash

PREPARATION TIME 10 MINUTES COOKING TIME 15 MINUTES SERVES 4

Thinly slice 1 large brown onion. Coarsely grate 1kg potatoes; stir in 1 teaspoon salt. Squeeze moisture from potato. Mix in onion; cook a quarter of the mixture at a time on heated oiled flat plate, turning until browned.

per serving 0.3g total fat (0g saturated fat); 711kJ (170 cal); 32.4g carbohydrate; 6.2g protein; 4.4g fibre

barbecued pizza trio

PREPARATION TIME 1 HOUR (PLUS STANDING TIME) COOKING TIME 20 MINUTES MAKES 3 THIN PIZZAS

This dough recipe makes enough for three thin pizza bases, and each of our topping recipes makes enough to cover one pizza base. We cut each pizza into five slices when serving.

2 teaspoons (7g) dry yeast
½ teaspoon white sugar
¾ cup (180ml) warm water
2 cups (300g) plain flour
1 teaspoon coarse cooking salt
2 tablespoons olive oil
cooking-oil spray
1 tablespoon olive oil, extra

MUSHROOM AND OLIVE
2 flat mushrooms (160g),
  sliced thickly
170g asparagus, trimmed
⅓ cup (85g) bottled tomato
  pasta sauce
2 tablespoons seeded black olives
1 tablespoon drained baby
  capers, rinsed

TOMATO AND BOCCONCINI
3 baby eggplants (180g), sliced
  thinly lengthways
1 tablespoon basil pesto
2 teaspoons olive oil
2 medium egg tomatoes (150g),
  sliced thinly
150g bocconcini, sliced thinly
12 fresh basil leaves, torn

POTATO AND PINE NUT
4 baby new potatoes (160g),
  sliced thinly
2 teaspoons finely chopped
  fresh rosemary
30g baby spinach leaves
⅓ cup (25g) flaked parmesan
1 tablespoon roasted pine nuts

1 To make pizza dough, combine yeast, sugar and the water in small bowl; cover, stand in warm place about 10 minutes or until frothy.

2 Combine yeast mixture, flour, salt and oil in large bowl; mix to a soft dough.

3 Knead dough on floured surface until elastic. Place dough in oiled large bowl, cover; stand in warm place about 1 hour or until doubled in size.

4 Meanwhile, preheat covered barbecue. Prepare toppings.

5 Knead dough on floured surface until smooth. Divide dough into thirds. Roll each piece to form 16cm x 40cm pizza base.

6 Layer two pieces of foil, large enough to fit one portion of dough. Spray top of foil with cooking-oil spray. Place one portion of dough on top of foil; repeat so that all three pizza bases sit on double layer of foil.

7 Place pizzas, on foil, on grill plate; cook, covered, using indirect heat, about 4 minutes or until underneath is browned lightly. (If dough puffs up, flatten quickly with an egg slide.)

8 Remove pizza bases from barbecue; close cover. Turn pizza bases over on foil; brush cooked side with extra oil then top with selected toppings, as directed below. Return pizzas to barbecue on foil; cover barbecue, cook 5 minutes or until well browned underneath and crisp.

MUSHROOM AND OLIVE Cook mushrooms and asparagus on heated oiled grill plate until tender. Spread pizza base with pasta sauce. Top with mushrooms, asparagus, olives and capers.
per slice 3.4g total fat (0.5g saturated fat); 539kJ (129 cal); 18.5g carbohydrate; 4.6g protein; 2.6g fibre

TOMATO AND BOCCONCINI Cook eggplant on heated oiled grill plate until tender. Spread pizza base with combined pesto and oil. Top with tomato, eggplant and cheese. Serve sprinkled with basil.
per slice 11.2g total fat (4g saturated fat); 853kJ (204 cal); 16.3g carbohydrate; 8.6g protein; 2.3g fibre

POTATO AND PINE NUT Cook potato on heated oiled grill plate until tender. Sprinkle pizza base with rosemary. Top with potato, spinach, cheese and nuts.
per slice 6.8g total fat (1.6g saturated fat); 681kJ (163 cal); 18.8g carbohydrate; 5.5g protein; 1.7g fibre

TIP Cooking pizza on a covered barbecue imparts a delicious smoky flavour similar to that of pizza made in a wood-fired oven, but this recipe can be cooked in your oven, too. Place topping of your choice on the uncooked pizza base then bake in a very hot oven (240°C/220°C fan-forced) until browned.

A chilled soup originating in the southern Spanish province of Andalusia, gazpacho, like other peasant soups, makes clever use of a garden's abundance of overripe vegetables.

grilled tomato and red capsicum gazpacho

PREPARATION TIME 30 MINUTES COOKING TIME 25 MINUTES (PLUS REFRIGERATION TIME) SERVES 4

3 medium red capsicums (600g)

6 medium egg tomatoes (450g),
   halved, seeded

1 medium red onion (170g),
   sliced thickly

4 cloves garlic, unpeeled

2 lebanese cucumbers (260g),
   seeded, chopped coarsely

2 tablespoons red wine vinegar

415ml can tomato juice

1 tablespoon coarsely chopped
   fresh flat-leaf parsley

¼ cup (60ml) cold water

PARMESAN CROUTONS

20g butter, melted

1 tablespoon olive oil

1 tablespoon finely grated parmesan

3 slices white bread (135g),
   crusts removed, quartered

1 Quarter capsicums, discard seeds and membranes. Roast under grill or in very hot oven, skin-side up, until skin blisters and blackens. Cover capsicum in plastic or paper for 5 minutes; peel away skin, chop coarsely.

2 Cook tomato, onion and garlic in heated oiled grill pan until tender. When cool enough to handle, peel garlic.

3 Blend or process capsicum, tomato, onion, garlic, cucumber, vinegar, juice and parsley, in batches, until gazpacho is smooth. Transfer to large bowl, cover; refrigerate about 3 hours or until cold.

4 Meanwhile, make parmesan croutons.

5 Stir the cold water into gazpacho. Serve chilled gazpacho sprinkled with croutons and extra chopped parsley.

PARMESAN CROUTONS Combine butter, oil and cheese in small bowl; add bread, turn to coat in mixture. Cook croutons in heated oiled grill pan until browned both sides.

per serving 10.9g total fat (4g saturated fat); 1994kJ (477 cal); 31.9g carbohydrate; 9.1g protein; 6.6g fibre

Whole or quartered salted lemons preserved in a mixture of olive oil and lemon juice are a North African specialty, and are added to tagines to infuse them with a rich, salty-sour flavour. A tablespoon of rinsed, finely chopped preserved lemon rind stirred into a cup of thick yogurt is excellent dolloped over a curry or stew.

grilled haloumi with pumpkin and pistachio couscous

PREPARATION TIME 35 MINUTES COOKING TIME 30 MINUTES SERVES 4

We used the Jarrahdale pumpkin variety for this recipe.

1 cup (250ml) vegetable stock

⅔ cup (160ml) water

1 tablespoon finely grated lemon rind

⅓ cup (80ml) lemon juice

60g cold butter

1½ cups (300g) couscous

1 tablespoon olive oil

1 medium red onion (170g), chopped finely

1 clove garlic, crushed

2 teaspoons sweet smoked paprika

1 teaspoon ground turmeric

1 teaspoon ground cumin

½ teaspoon cayenne pepper

½ cup (70g) roasted pistachios

¼ cup (50g) finely chopped preserved lemon

¼ cup finely chopped fresh flat-leaf parsley

¼ cup finely chopped fresh mint

600g piece pumpkin, trimmed, sliced thinly

180g packet haloumi cheese

1 Bring stock, the water, rind, juice and butter to a boil in large saucepan. Remove from heat; stir in couscous. Cover; stand about 5 minutes or until liquid is absorbed, fluffing occasionally with fork.

2 Meanwhile, heat oil in medium frying pan; cook onion, garlic and spices, stirring, until onion softens.

3 Add onion mixture to couscous with nuts, lemon and herbs; toss gently to combine. Cover to keep warm.

4 Cook pumpkin in heated oiled grill pan about 10 minutes or until tender.

5 Slice cheese lengthways into four pieces; cut each piece into triangles. Cook cheese in same oiled grill pan until browned both sides.

6 Serve couscous topped with pumpkin and cheese, and sprinkled with more coarsely chopped parsley.

per serving 34.8g total fat (15.3g saturated fat); 3018kJ (722 cal); 71.7g carbohydrate; 27.2g protein; 5.3g fibre

Za'atar, a blend of roasted dry spices, is easy to make, but the prepared mixture, consisting of sesame seeds, marjoram, thyme and sumac, can be purchased in all Middle Eastern food shops and some delicatessens. Try it sprinkled on warm toast that's been spread with ricotta.

spicy ratatouille

PREPARATION TIME 15 MINUTES COOKING TIME 30 MINUTES SERVES 4

2 medium green capsicums (400g)
1 medium eggplant (300g),
  chopped coarsely
2 medium zucchini (240g),
  chopped coarsely
1 tablespoon olive oil
2 medium brown onions (300g),
  chopped coarsely
4 cloves garlic, sliced thinly
1 tablespoon finely chopped
  fresh thyme
1 teaspoon dried chilli flakes
700g bottled tomato pasta sauce
½ cup (125ml) water
½ cup coarsely chopped fresh basil

1 Quarter capsicums, discard seeds and membranes. Roast under grill or in very hot oven, skin-side up, until skin blisters and blackens. Cover capsicum pieces in plastic or paper for 5 minutes; peel away skin, chop coarsely.
2 Meanwhile, cook eggplant and zucchini, in batches, in heated oiled grill pan until tender.
3 Heat oil in large saucepan; cook onion, garlic, thyme and chilli, stirring occasionally, until onion softens.
4 Add capsicum, eggplant, zucchini, sauce and the water; simmer, uncovered, 5 minutes. Remove from heat; stir in basil.
per serving 6.5g total fat (0.8g saturated fat); 815kJ (195 cal); 24.4g carbohydrate; 6.5g protein; 8.3g fibre

potato, spinach and za'atar frittatas

PREPARATION TIME 20 MINUTES (PLUS STANDING TIME) COOKING TIME 40 MINUTES SERVES 4

2 tablespoons olive oil
1 tablespoon za'atar
4 medium potatoes (800g),
  sliced thinly
2 cloves garlic, unpeeled
6 eggs
½ cup (125ml) cream
40g baby spinach leaves
1 tablespoon roasted sesame seeds

1 Grease four shallow 11cm pie dishes; line bases with baking paper.
2 Combine oil, za'atar and potato in medium bowl.
3 Cook potato mixture and garlic on heated oiled flat plate until almost tender.
4 Squeeze cooked garlic into medium jug; discard skins. Whisk in eggs and cream. Divide half the potato mixture among dishes; top with half the egg mixture, then spinach, remaining potato mixture and remaining egg mixture.
5 Cook frittatas on heated flat plate, covered, about 20 minutes or until almost firm. Stand 10 minutes to allow to firm. Serve frittatas sprinkled with sesame seeds.
per serving 32.3g total fat (12.8g saturated fat); 1906kJ (456 cal); 24.3g carbohydrate; 15.7g protein; 3.6g fibre

In early times, rosemary grew wild in most kitchen gardens so it found its way into many of our favourite vegetable dishes. However, its flavour marries well with meats, too, especially if teamed with lemon and garlic.

grilled vegetables with garlic rosemary dressing

PREPARATION TIME 30 MINUTES COOKING TIME 30 MINUTES SERVES 4

1 medium red capsicum (200g)

1 medium yellow capsicum (200g)

¼ cup (60ml) olive oil

1 clove garlic, crushed

1 teaspoon finely grated lemon rind

2 teaspoons finely chopped
  fresh rosemary

1 medium red onion (170g), cut
  into wedges

2 small leeks (400g), trimmed, cut
  into 2cm pieces

1 medium eggplant (300g),
  sliced thickly

2 medium zucchini (240g),
  sliced thickly

4 flat mushrooms (320g), quartered

3 cloves garlic, unpeeled

⅓ cup (100g) mayonnaise

1 tablespoon lemon juice

1 Quarter capsicums, discard seeds and membranes. Roast under grill or in very hot oven, skin-side up, until skin blisters and blackens. Cover capsicum pieces in plastic or paper for 5 minutes; peel away skin, slice thickly.

2 Combine oil, crushed garlic, rind and half the rosemary in small bowl.

3 Brush onion, leek, eggplant, zucchini, mushrooms and unpeeled garlic with oil mixture; cook vegetables, in batches, on heated oiled grill plate until tender.

4 Squeeze cooked garlic into small jug; discard skins. Whisk in remaining rosemary, mayonnaise and juice. Serve vegetables with dressing.

per serving 22.8g total fat (2.9g saturated fat); 1325kJ (317 cal); 16.9g carbohydrate; 7.9g protein; 8.4g fibre

Black beans, also known as turtle beans, are not the same as chinese black beans, which are fermented soy beans. A common ingredient in Caribbean and Latin American soups, salsas and salads, black beans can be found in most health food stores and large greengrocers.

chunky black bean and grilled corn salad with cheesy nachos

PREPARATION TIME 20 MINUTES (PLUS STANDING TIME) COOKING TIME 1 HOUR SERVES 4

¾ cup (150g) dried black beans
1 medium red capsicum (200g)
2 trimmed corn cobs (500g)
1 small red onion (100g),
  chopped finely
1 fresh long red chilli, chopped finely
2 cloves garlic, crushed
1 tablespoon finely grated lime rind
½ cup (125ml) lime juice
1 teaspoon ground cumin
⅓ cup coarsely chopped
  fresh coriander
2 medium avocados (500g),
  chopped coarsely
230g packet corn chips
1⅓ cups (160g) coarsely
  grated cheddar
⅓ cup (80g) sour cream

1 Place beans in medium bowl, cover with water; stand overnight. Rinse under cold water; drain. Cook beans in medium saucepan of boiling water, uncovered, until tender; drain. Rinse under cold water; drain.
2 Quarter capsicum, discard seeds and membranes. Roast under grill or in very hot oven, skin-side up, until skin blisters and blackens. Cover capsicum pieces in plastic or paper for 5 minutes; peel away skin, chop coarsely.
3 Cook corn on heated oiled grill plate until browned lightly and tender; cut kernels from cobs. Combine beans, capsicum, corn, onion, chilli, garlic, rind, juice, cumin and coriander in large bowl. Add avocado; mix gently into salad.
4 Preheat grill.
5 Divide chips and cheese among ovenproof serving plates; grill until cheese melts. Top with salad; serve with sour cream.
per serving 60.2g total fat (25g saturated fat); 4055kJ (970 cal); 67.3g carbohydrate; 31.6g protein; 18.6g fibre

Tofu, or bean curd, is sold as soft, firm, fried or dried in sheets. Here, firm silken tofu (so-called because of the way it's made, by straining soy milk through silk), mashed with spicy onion, is shaped into a burger made even tastier by the accompanying hummus and fresh herbs.

tofu and vegie burger

PREPARATION TIME 20 MINUTES (PLUS STANDING TIME) COOKING TIME 20 MINUTES (PLUS REFRIGERATION TIME) SERVES 4

300g firm silken tofu

1 tablespoon olive oil

1 medium brown onion (150g), chopped finely

2 cloves garlic, crushed

¼ teaspoon sweet paprika

1 teaspoon ground turmeric

2 teaspoons ground coriander

1 small zucchini (90g), grated coarsely

2 cups (140g) fresh breadcrumbs

¾ cup (190g) hummus

¼ cup (70g) greek-style yogurt

1 loaf turkish bread (430g)

⅓ cup coarsely chopped fresh mint

½ cup coarsely chopped fresh flat-leaf parsley

1 green onion, sliced thinly

30g snow pea sprouts, trimmed

1 Pat tofu dry with absorbent paper. Spread tofu, in single layer, on absorbent-paper-lined tray; cover tofu with more paper, stand 20 minutes.

2 Meanwhile, heat oil in medium frying pan; cook brown onion and garlic, stirring, until onion softens. Add spices; cook, stirring, until fragrant.

3 Combine onion mixture in large bowl with tofu, zucchini and breadcrumbs; shape into four patties. Cover; refrigerate 30 minutes.

4 Meanwhile, combine hummus and yogurt in small bowl.

5 Cut bread into four pieces. Split each piece in half horizontally; toast cut sides in heated oiled grill pan.

6 Cook patties in same oiled grill pan until browned both sides and hot.

7 Spread bread with hummus mixture; sandwich combined mint, parsley and green onion, patties and sprouts between bread pieces.

per serving 24.1g total fat (4.6g saturated fat); 2880kJ (689 cal); 81.5g carbohydrate; 30.2g protein; 11.7g fibre

The Spanish word for "sauce", salsas can be fresh or cooked, smooth or chunky, eaten also as salads or dips, and range in taste from very mild to fiery. Increasingly, salsas have become contemporary mainstream concepts, quite unlike any of their Spanish or Mexican ancestors.

paprika and parmesan polenta with walnut and capsicum salsa

PREPARATION TIME 20 MINUTES COOKING TIME 45 MINUTES (PLUS REFRIGERATION TIME) SERVES 6

20g butter

2 medium brown onions (300g), sliced thinly

1 tablespoon brown sugar

1 litre (4 cups) water

1⅓ cups (225g) polenta

2 teaspoons smoked paprika

1 tablespoon red wine vinegar

1 cup (80g) coarsely grated parmesan

WALNUT AND CAPSICUM SALSA

2 large red capsicums (700g)

1½ cups (150g) roasted walnuts, chopped coarsely

1 tablespoon red wine vinegar

¼ cup (60ml) walnut oil

1 clove garlic, crushed

½ cup coarsely chopped fresh flat-leaf parsley

1 Melt butter in medium frying pan; cook onion, stirring, about 5 minutes or until softened. Add sugar and 2 tablespoons of the water; cook about 2 minutes or until onion caramelises. Cover to keep warm.

2 Oil deep 22cm-round cake pan. Bring remaining water to a boil in medium saucepan. Gradually add polenta and paprika, stirring constantly. Simmer, stirring, about 8 minutes or until polenta thickens. Stir in vinegar and cheese then spread half the polenta into pan. Spread onion mixture over polenta, spread remaining polenta over onion. Cover; refrigerate 3 hours or until firm.

3 Meanwhile, make walnut and capsicum salsa.

4 Turn polenta onto board; cut into six wedges. Cook polenta, both sides, on heated oiled grill plate until browned lightly and hot. Serve polenta with salsa.

WALNUT AND CAPSICUM SALSA Quarter capsicums, discard seeds and membranes. Roast under grill or in very hot oven, skin-side up, until skin blisters and blackens. Cover capsicum pieces in plastic or paper for 5 minutes; peel away skin, chop coarsely. Combine capsicum in small bowl with remaining ingredients.

per serving 51.8g total fat (10.6g saturated fat); 3210kJ (768 cal); 51.9g carbohydrate; 21.2g protein; 7.1g fibre

vegies on the side

warm potato and kumara salad

PREPARATION TIME 20 MINUTES COOKING TIME 30 MINUTES SERVES 4

750g kipfler potatoes, halved lengthways
500g kumara, chopped coarsely
⅓ cup (80ml) olive oil
1 small red onion (100g), sliced thinly
¼ cup finely chopped fresh dill
¼ cup finely chopped fresh basil
¼ cup (60ml) lemon juice
2 tablespoons drained capers, rinsed, chopped finely
1 tablespoon wholegrain mustard
1 clove garlic, crushed

1 Boil, steam or microwave potato and kumara,
separately, until tender; drain.
2 Preheat grill.
3 Place potato and kumara, in single layer, on oiled
oven trays. Brush potato and kumara with a little of
the oil; grill, in batches, until browned.
4 Meanwhile, combine remaining oil, onion, dill,
basil, juice, capers, mustard and garlic in large bowl.
Add potato and kumara; mix gently.
*per serving 18.7g total fat (2.6g saturated fat); 1605kJ (384 cal);
42.8g carbohydrate; 7.3g protein; 6.5g fibre*

grilled asian vegetables

PREPARATION TIME 10 MINUTES COOKING TIME 10 MINUTES SERVES 4

400g baby buk choy, trimmed, halved lengthways
2 tablespoons peanut oil
175g broccolini, halved
100g snow peas, trimmed
200g baby corn, halved lengthways
2 tablespoons mirin
1 tablespoon vegetarian oyster sauce
1 tablespoon light soy sauce
1 clove garlic, crushed
1 teaspoon white sugar
½ teaspoon sesame oil

1 Boil, steam or microwave buk choy until wilted;
drain. Brush with half the peanut oil; cook on heated
oiled flat plate until tender.
2 Combine broccolini, peas and corn in large bowl
with remaining peanut oil; mix well. Cook vegetables,
in batches, on same flat plate until tender.
3 Meanwhile, combine mirin, sauces, garlic, sugar
and sesame oil in same bowl; add vegetables, mix well.
*per serving 10.7g total fat (1.8g saturated fat); 811kJ (194 cal);
13.4g carbohydrate; 6.5g protein; 6.1g fibre*

TIP "Vegetarian" oyster sauce is made from blended
mushrooms and soy, and is available from health food
stores and some supermarkets.

grilled asparagus with tomato

PREPARATION TIME 10 MINUTES COOKING TIME 20 MINUTES SERVES 4

You need four bunches of asparagus for this recipe.

¼ cup (60ml) olive oil
¼ cup (60ml) white wine vinegar
2 teaspoons fresh lemon thyme leaves
2 cloves garlic, crushed
2 large red onions (600g), cut into wedges
680g asparagus, trimmed, halved
250g cherry tomatoes, halved

1 Combine oil, vinegar, thyme, garlic and onion in large bowl. Drain onion; reserve vinegar mixture in bowl.
2 Cook onion on heated oiled flat plate until soft and browned lightly.
3 Meanwhile, cook asparagus and tomato, in batches, on flat plate until tender.
4 Combine vegetables in bowl with reserved vinegar mixture.

per serving 14.1g total fat (1.9g saturated fat); 895kJ (214 cal); 12g carbohydrate; 6.8g protein; 5.8g fibre

marinated mixed mushrooms

PREPARATION TIME 15 MINUTES (PLUS REFRIGERATION TIME)
COOKING TIME 10 MINUTES SERVES 4

2 cloves garlic, crushed
4cm piece fresh ginger (20g), grated
⅓ cup (80ml) light soy sauce
2 tablespoons mirin
2 tablespoons sake
2 tablespoons peanut oil
1 tablespoon white sugar
200g oyster mushrooms
200g shiitake mushrooms
200g button mushrooms
200g swiss brown mushrooms
200g enoki mushrooms
4 green onions, sliced diagonally

1 Combine garlic, ginger, sauce, mirin, sake, oil and sugar in large bowl; add mushrooms, mix gently. Cover; refrigerate 2 hours.
2 Drain mushrooms; reserve marinade in bowl.
3 Cook mushrooms, in batches, on heated oiled flat plate until tender.
4 Combine mushrooms and onion in bowl with reserved marinade.

per serving 9.8g total fat (1.7g saturated fat); 890kJ (213 cal); 14.9g carbohydrate; 9.2g protein; 7.7g fibre

seafood

Nothing beats the taste of seafood cooked on a barbecue

prawn and chorizo skewers with bean and tomato salad

PREPARATION TIME 25 MINUTES (PLUS REFRIGERATION TIME) COOKING TIME 10 MINUTES SERVES 4

24 uncooked medium
  king prawns (1kg)
4 cloves garlic, crushed
2 tablespoons olive oil
150g green beans, trimmed, halved
3 medium egg tomatoes (225g),
  quartered
2 tablespoons roasted pine nuts
¼ cup coarsely chopped fresh
  flat-leaf parsley
8 x 20cm stalks fresh rosemary
2 chorizo sausages (340g),
  sliced thickly

LIME MUSTARD DRESSING
2 tablespoons olive oil
2 tablespoons lime juice
1 tablespoon wholegrain mustard
2 cloves garlic, crushed

1 Shell and devein prawns, leaving tails intact. Combine prawns in medium bowl with garlic and oil. Cover; refrigerate 3 hours or overnight.
2 Combine ingredients for lime mustard dressing in screw-top jar; shake well.
3 Meanwhile, boil, steam or microwave beans until just tender; drain. Rinse under cold water; drain. Combine beans in medium bowl with tomato, nuts, parsley and dressing.
4 Drain prawns, discard marinade. Remove leaves from bottom two-thirds of each rosemary stalk; thread prawns and chorizo, alternately, onto rosemary skewers. Cook skewers in heated oiled grill pan until prawns are changed in colour and chorizo is browned.
per serving 49.9g total fat (12.3g saturated fat); 2730kJ (653 cal); 5.4g carbohydrate; 45g protein; 3.4g fibre

USING
SKEWERS

rosemary skewers

skewering asparagus

skewering potatoes

cinnamon skewers

sealing stuffing with a skewer

using skewers to hold shape

skewering onions

lemon grass skewers

rosemary skewers

Thread chopped meat, seafood, poultry or vegetables onto long stalks of fresh rosemary to infuse the food with flavour. Use sturdy, coarse stalks so they hold the food, and remove about two-thirds of the leaves from the bottom part of each stalk. Sharpen end of stalks to make it easier to pierce meat or vegetables.

skewering asparagus

Use bamboo skewers for easy turning of asparagus, but make sure you soak them in cold water for at least an hour before using to prevent them splintering and scorching. Push one skewer, about a third of the way up from the base, crossways through 4 or 5 trimmed asparagus spears; push a second skewer through the spears about a third of the way down from the top. Brush asparagus with olive oil; cook on heated oiled grill plate, turning every 2 minutes, for about 10 minutes or until asparagus is browned and tender.

skewering potatoes

To cook whole potatoes faster and make them easy to turn and move around, skewer two or three potatoes on long thick metal skewers. The metal will conduct heat through the centre of the potatoes, thus helping them to cook faster.

cinnamon skewers

Cinnamon sticks are good for skewering and roasting marshmallows or slender sections of kumara.

sealing stuffing with a skewer

Thread strong wooden toothpicks or metal poultry pins through the edges of any stuffed meat, poultry or fish to seal the flaps and keep filling secure during cooking.

using skewers to hold shape

Secure tails of loin chops to meat with skewers to hold shape during cooking. Thread long skewers through body of flattened quail or spatchcock to keep them flat and ensure even cooking.

skewering onions

To cook onion pieces easily and evenly on the barbecue, skewer wedges through all layers. This holds them together even when they are turned.

lemon grass skewers

Lemon grass sticks are good for chunks of fish and beef. Peel some of the brownish leaves from the top; cut base of stick into a point and push through meat.

Based on a recipe from the Indian coastal province of Kerala, this delicious grilled fish is even better with the tangy lime pickle yogurt spooned over the top.

seared salmon kerala-style with lime pickle yogurt

PREPARATION TIME 20 MINUTES COOKING TIME 15 MINUTES (PLUS REFRIGERATION TIME) SERVES 4

2 teaspoons coriander seeds
1 teaspoon cumin seeds
2 cardamom pods, bruised
1 cinnamon stick
1 teaspoon ground turmeric
½ teaspoon chilli powder
2 tablespoons peanut oil
2 cloves garlic, crushed
4 x 265g salmon cutlets
100g baby spinach leaves

LIME PICKLE YOGURT
½ cup (140g) yogurt
2 tablespoons lime pickle,
  chopped finely

1 Dry-fry coriander, cumin, cardamom and cinnamon in small heated frying pan, stirring, over medium heat until fragrant. Stir in turmeric and chilli powder; remove from heat.
2 Crush spices, using mortar and pestle, until ground finely; transfer to large bowl. Stir in oil and garlic, add fish; turn fish to coat in marinade. Cover; refrigerate 30 minutes.
3 Meanwhile, combine ingredients for lime pickle yogurt in small bowl.
4 Cook fish in heated oiled grill pan. Serve fish with spinach and yogurt.
per serving 29.3g total fat (6.7g saturated fat); 2082kJ (498 cal); 3.9g carbohydrate; 54.1g protein; 1.1g fibre

Fried shallots are a staple in the Thai kitchen, used variously as an ingredient when stir-frying, sprinkled over just-cooked dishes or presented as a condiment at the table. Here we've used them to add crunch to the burger mixture. They can be purchased already made from Asian grocery stores or you can make your own; they'll keep for months if stored tightly sealed.

thai fish burger

PREPARATION TIME 20 MINUTES COOKING TIME 15 MINUTES SERVES 4

We used blue-eye here, but any firm white fish fillets can be used.

500g blue-eye fillets,
  chopped coarsely
1 tablespoon fish sauce
1 tablespoon kecap manis
1 clove garlic, quartered
1 fresh small red thai chilli,
  chopped coarsely
50g green beans, trimmed,
  chopped coarsely
¼ cup (20g) fried shallots
¼ cup coarsely chopped
  fresh coriander
60g baby spinach leaves
1 lebanese cucumber (130g),
  seeded, sliced thinly
1 tablespoon lime juice
2 teaspoons brown sugar
2 teaspoons fish sauce, extra
4 hamburger buns (360g)
⅓ cup (80ml) sweet chilli sauce

1 Blend or process fish, sauce, kecap manis, garlic and chilli until smooth. Combine fish mixture in large bowl with beans, shallots and coriander; shape into four patties.
2 Cook patties on heated oiled flat plate about 15 minutes or until cooked.
3 Combine spinach, cucumber, juice, sugar and extra sauce in medium bowl.
4 Split buns in half; toast cut-sides. Sandwich salad, patties and sweet chilli sauce between bun halves.
per serving 5.3g total fat (0.7g saturated fat); 1722kJ (412 cal); 55.2g carbohydrate; 32g protein; 5.7g fibre

seafood antipasto

PREPARATION TIME 25 MINUTES (PLUS REFRIGERATION TIME) COOKING TIME 20 MINUTES SERVES 4

12 uncooked large king prawns (840g)

8 sardine fillets (360g)

8 whole cleaned baby octopus (720g)

2 cloves garlic, crushed

2 tablespoons olive oil

440g loaf ciabatta, sliced thickly

170g asparagus, halved lengthways

200g grape tomatoes

1 cup (150g) seeded kalamata olives

250g haloumi cheese, sliced
  lengthways into 8 pieces

GARLIC CHILLI DRESSING

4 cloves garlic, crushed

1 tablespoon finely grated lime rind

¼ cup (60ml) lime juice

2 fresh small red thai chillies,
  chopped finely

1 Combine ingredients for garlic chilli dressing in screw-top jar; shake well.

2 Shell and devein prawns, leaving heads and tails intact. Combine prawns in large bowl with sardines, octopus, half the garlic and half the oil. Cover; refrigerate 3 hours or overnight.

3 Meanwhile, combine remaining garlic and oil in small bowl; brush bread slices, both sides, with garlic oil. Toast bread, both sides, on heated oiled flat plate.

4 Cook asparagus, tomatoes, olives and cheese, in batches, on flat plate, until asparagus is tender.

5 Cook seafood, in batches, on flat plate until cooked as desired; drizzle with dressing. Serve with vegetables and cheese.

per serving 51.1g total fat (15.4g saturated fat); 4840kJ (1158 cal); 63.2g carbohydrate; 108g protein; 6.2g fibre

salmon with macadamia mayonnaise

PREPARATION TIME 10 MINUTES COOKING TIME 10 MINUTES SERVES 4

2 egg yolks

½ teaspoon coarse cooking salt

½ teaspoon mustard powder

2 tablespoons lemon juice

½ cup (125ml) light olive oil

⅓ cup (45g) roasted macadamias,
  chopped coarsely

4 x 200g salmon fillets

1 Preheat grill.

2 To make macadamia mayonnaise, combine egg yolks in medium bowl with salt, mustard and half the juice. Gradually add oil in thin, steady stream, whisking constantly until mixture thickens. Whisk in remaining juice and nuts.

3 Grill salmon, skin-side up, until skin is crisp; turn, grill until cooked as desired. Serve with macadamia mayonnaise.

per serving 54.1g total fat (9.2g saturated fat); 2725kJ (652 cal); 0.8g carbohydrate; 41.5g protein; 0.7g fibre

For a simple yet stylish dish, try this splendid antipasto. The seafood can be prepared the night before, as can the garlic chilli dressing.

You can use uncooked moreton bay bugs or fresh scampi in this recipe if balmain bugs are out of season.

bugs with garlic herbed butter

PREPARATION TIME 30 MINUTES COOKING TIME 20 MINUTES SERVES 4

8 uncooked balmain bugs (1.6kg)
4 large flat mushrooms (360g)
100g curly endive, chopped coarsely

HERB BUTTER
125g butter, softened
2 teaspoons finely grated lemon rind
2 tablespoons lemon juice
2 tablespoons finely chopped
  fresh chives
2 tablespoons coarsely chopped
  fresh flat-leaf parsley
2 tablespoons coarsely chopped
  fresh tarragon
1 clove garlic, crushed

1 Place bugs upside down on board; cut tail from body, discard body. Using scissors, cut soft shell from underneath tails to expose meat; cut tails in half lengthways. Discard back vein.

2 Make herbed butter.

3 Melt half the herb butter in small saucepan. Brush mushrooms with half the melted butter; cook on heated oiled grill plate until tender.

4 Brush bugs with remaining melted butter mixture; cook on grill plate.

5 Serve endive and mushrooms with bug halves; top with remaining herb butter.

HERB BUTTER Beat butter, rind and juice in small bowl with electric mixer until light and fluffy. Stir in herbs and garlic.

per serving 27.1g total fat (17.1g saturated fat); 1584kJ (379 cal); 2.1g carbohydrate; 30.4g protein; 3.2g fibre

Lime is the perfect acidic component for a seafood dressing. Combined with chilli, pineapple and mint to create a clean, fresh foil for the richness of the lobster, or teamed with fish sauce and palm sugar to impart piquancy to a grilled squid salad, it's the zesty tang of lime that adds life to the food.

lobster tails with lime butter and pineapple mint salsa

PREPARATION TIME 20 MINUTES COOKING TIME 10 MINUTES SERVES 4

100g butter

1 teaspoon finely grated lime rind

1 fresh small red thai chilli,
  chopped finely

2cm piece fresh ginger (10g), grated

4 uncooked small lobster tails in
  shells (660g)

PINEAPPLE MINT SALSA

1 small pineapple (900g),
  chopped coarsely

2 tablespoons lime juice

½ cup finely chopped fresh mint

1 fresh long red chilli, chopped finely

1 Combine ingredients for pineapple mint salsa in medium bowl.

2 Melt butter in small saucepan; cook rind, chilli and ginger, stirring, 2 minutes.

3 Using scissors, cut soft shell from underneath lobster tails to expose meat; cut lobster tails in half lengthways. Brush with butter mixture; cook, in batches, on heated oiled grill plate until cooked through. Serve with salsa.

per serving 21.9g total fat (13.8g saturated fat); 1538kJ (368 cal); 10.1g carbohydrate; 31.1g protein; 3.1g fibre

squid salad with garlic lime dressing

PREPARATION TIME 25 MINUTES COOKING TIME 10 MINUTES SERVES 4

1kg cleaned squid hoods

1 fresh long red chilli, chopped finely

1 tablespoon peanut oil

500g rocket, trimmed

150g snow peas, sliced thinly

227g can drained water chestnuts,
  rinsed, sliced thinly

½ cup loosely packed fresh
  coriander leaves

½ cup loosely packed fresh
  mint leaves

GARLIC LIME DRESSING

¼ cup (60ml) lime juice

2 cloves garlic, crushed

2 tablespoons fish sauce

2 tablespoons grated palm sugar

2 green onions, sliced thinly

1 fresh long red chilli, chopped finely

1 tablespoon peanut oil

1 Combine ingredients for garlic lime dressing in screw-top jar; shake well.

2 Cut squid down centre to open out; score inside in diagonal pattern then cut into thick strips.

3 Combine squid, chilli and oil in medium bowl. Combine remaining ingredients for salad in large bowl.

4 Cook squid, in batches, in heated oiled grill pan; combine in bowl with salad and dressing.

per serving 11.8g total fat (2.1g saturated fat); 1133kJ (271 cal); 15.3g carbohydrate; 23.9g protein; 4.6g fibre

grilled tuna with japanese chilled soba salad

PREPARATION TIME 20 MINUTES COOKING TIME 10 MINUTES (PLUS REFRIGERATION TIME) SERVES 4

250g soba

¼ cup (70g) pickled pink ginger,
  sliced thinly

4 green onions, sliced thinly

4 x 175g tuna steaks

1 sheet toasted nori, shredded

SOY MIRIN DRESSING

¼ cup (60ml) light soy sauce

⅓ cup (80ml) mirin

1 tablespoon rice vinegar

2 tablespoons cooking sake

1 teaspoon sesame oil

1 teaspoon wasabi paste

1 Cook noodles in large saucepan of boiling water, uncovered, until tender; drain. Rinse under cold water, drain thoroughly.

2 Combine ingredients for soy mirin dressing in screw-top jar; shake well.

3 Combine cold noodles, ginger and onion in large bowl, add three-quarters of the dressing; mix gently. Cover; refrigerate until chilled.

4 Cook tuna, both sides, in heated oiled grill pan until just cooked (do not overcook or tuna will dry out).

5 Serve tuna drizzled with remaining dressing, topped with nori. Serve with soba salad.

per serving 11.9g total fat (4.3g saturated fat); 2207kJ (528 cal); 45.1g carbohydrate; 52.1g protein; 2.8g fibre

snapper and chilli-salted potato slices with capsicum remoulade

PREPARATION TIME 25 MINUTES COOKING TIME 30 MINUTES SERVES 4

3 large potatoes (900g), unpeeled,
  cut into 1cm slices

¼ cup (60ml) olive oil

1 tablespoon fried shallots

½ teaspoon dried chilli flakes

2 teaspoons sea salt

4 x 275g snapper fillets

¼ cup (35g) plain flour

CAPSICUM REMOULADE

⅓ cup (85g) char-grilled capsicum,
  drained, sliced thinly

⅓ cup (100g) mayonnaise

1 tablespoon drained capers,
  rinsed, chopped finely

2 anchovy fillets, drained,
  chopped finely

1 tablespoon finely chopped
  fresh flat-leaf parsley

2 teaspoons lemon juice

1 Boil, steam or microwave potato until tender; drain. Combine in medium bowl with oil.

2 Meanwhile, crush shallots, chilli and salt finely using mortar and pestle.

3 Combine ingredients for capsicum remoulade in small bowl.

4 Coat fish in flour; shake off excess.

5 Cook potato slices, in batches, on heated oiled flat plate until browned both sides. Sprinkle with chilli salt; cover to keep warm.

6 Cook fish on flat plate until browned both sides and cooked through.

7 Serve fish with remoulade and potato.

per serving 28.2g total fat (4.7g saturated fat); 2880kJ (689 cal); 42.2g carbohydrate; 63.2g protein; 4.2g fibre

Soba is a spaghetti-like, pale brown noodle made from various proportions of wheat and buckwheat flours. Both fresh and dried soba can be found in Japanese food shops and some supermarkets.

Often sold by their Thai name of homm jiew, fried shallots are available from Asian grocery stores in jars or cellophane bags, and will keep for months if stored tightly sealed. They can be added to any number of Western dishes for a tasty bit of surprise crunch, as we have done here.

kaffir lime and lemon grass grilled trout

PREPARATION TIME 20 MINUTES COOKING TIME 45 MINUTES SERVES 6

10cm stick (20g) fresh lemon grass,
  chopped coarsely
4cm piece fresh ginger (20g),
  sliced thickly
2 cloves garlic, quartered
2 tablespoons peanut oil
1 tablespoon sweet chilli sauce
1 tablespoon lime juice
2 green onions, chopped finely
1 whole ocean trout (2.4kg)
1 lime, peeled, sliced thinly
10cm stick (20g) fresh lemon grass,
  sliced diagonally
1 kaffir lime leaf, shredded thinly
⅓ cup loosely packed fresh
  coriander leaves
1 lime, cut into wedges

1 Blend or process chopped lemon grass, ginger, garlic, oil, sauce and juice until smooth. Stir in onion.

2 Place long piece of baking paper on bench; place fish on paper. Fill cavity with lemon grass mixture.

3 Score fish three times both sides through thickest part of flesh; seal cuts with lime slices; sprinkle fish with sliced lemon grass and lime leaf. Fold paper over fish to completely enclose, then wrap fish tightly in foil.

4 Cook fish on heated oiled grill plate 25 minutes; turn, cook about 20 minutes or until cooked through.

5 Serve fish sprinkled with coriander; serve with lime wedges.

per serving 14.3g total fat (3g saturated fat); 1262kJ (302 cal); 1.2g carbohydrate; 41.4g protein; 0.7g fibre

barramundi with tomato, caper and walnut dressing

PREPARATION TIME 15 MINUTES COOKING TIME 20 MINUTES SERVES 4

4 x 185g barramundi fillets

**TOMATO, CAPER AND
WALNUT DRESSING**
250g cherry tomatoes
60g butter
1 tablespoon finely grated lemon rind
2 teaspoons lemon juice
1 teaspoon drained capers, rinsed,
  chopped finely
¼ cup (30g) finely chopped walnuts
½ cup coarsely chopped fresh
  flat-leaf parsley

1 Make tomato, caper and walnut dressing.

2 Cook fish on grill plate. Serve fish topped with dressing.

TOMATO, CAPER AND WALNUT DRESSING Cook tomatoes on heated oiled grill plate until tender. Melt butter in small saucepan; add tomatoes and remaining ingredients, stirring until hot.

per serving 19.8g total fat (9.2g saturated fat); 1471kJ (352 cal); 2g carbohydrate; 40.1g protein; 1.9g fibre

grilled scallops

scallops with fennel béchamel

PREPARATION TIME 15 MINUTES COOKING TIME 15 MINUTES SERVES 4
(MAKES 1 CUP SAUCE)

40g butter
1 baby fennel bulb (130g), trimmed, sliced thinly
2 tablespoons plain flour
1 cup (250ml) milk
24 scallops, roe removed (600g), on the half shell
1 tablespoon finely chopped fresh dill

1   Melt butter in small saucepan; cook fennel, stirring,
about 5 minutes or until fennel softens. Add flour; cook,
stirring, about 2 minutes or until mixture bubbles and
thickens. Gradually stir in milk; cook, stirring, until
béchamel boils and thickens.
2   Preheat grill.
3   Remove scallops from shells; rinse and dry shells.
Return scallops to shells; grill scallops about 5 minutes
or until cooked. Top scallops with béchamel; grill until
browned lightly. Sprinkle scallops with dill.
*per serving 11.8g total fat (7.3g saturated fat); 928kJ (222 cal);
8.6g carbohydrate; 20.4g protein; 0.7g fibre*

scallops with warm rocket pesto

PREPARATION TIME 15 MINUTES COOKING TIME 6 MINUTES SERVES 4
(MAKES ½ CUP PESTO)

40g baby rocket leaves
¼ cup (35g) roasted pistachios
1 clove garlic, quartered
1 teaspoon finely grated lemon rind
2 teaspoons lemon juice
¼ cup (60ml) olive oil
¼ cup (60ml) warm water
2 tablespoons finely grated parmesan
24 scallops, roe removed (600g), on the half shell

1   Blend or process rocket, nuts, garlic, rind and
juice until smooth. With motor operating, gradually
add oil in thin, steady stream until pesto is almost
smooth. Stir in the water and cheese.
2   Preheat grill.
3   Remove scallops from shells; rinse and dry
shells. Return scallops to shells; grill scallops about
5 minutes or until cooked. Top scallops with pesto;
grill until pesto bubbles.
*per serving 20.3g total fat (3.4g saturated fat); 1158kJ (277 cal);
2.6g carbohydrate; 20.7g protein; 1.1g fibre*

bacon and tomato scallops

PREPARATION TIME 15 MINUTES COOKING TIME 12 MINUTES SERVES 4

15g butter
3 bacon rashers (210g), rind removed, chopped finely
2 small egg tomatoes (120g), seeded, chopped finely
2 green onions, sliced thinly
24 scallops, roe removed (600g), on the half shell
⅓ cup (25g) coarsely grated parmesan

1 Melt butter in medium frying pan; cook bacon, stirring, about 5 minutes or until bacon is crisp. Remove from heat; stir in tomato and onion.
2 Preheat grill.
3 Remove scallops from shells; rinse and dry shells. Return scallops to shells; grill scallops about 5 minutes or until cooked. Top scallops with bacon mixture and cheese; grill until cheese melts.
per serving 9.9g total fat (5g saturated fat); 836kJ (200 cal); 2g carbohydrate; 25.5g protein; 0.5g fibre

spinach and mustard scallops

PREPARATION TIME 15 MINUTES COOKING TIME 15 MINUTES SERVES 4

20g butter
1 medium brown onion (150g), chopped finely
1 clove garlic, crushed
1½ teaspoons black mustard seeds
300g spinach, trimmed, shredded finely
⅔ cup (160ml) cream
24 scallops, roe removed (600g), on the half shell
½ cup (35g) stale breadcrumbs

1 Melt butter in medium frying pan; cook onion and garlic, stirring, about 5 minutes or until onion softens. Add seeds and spinach; cook, stirring, about 2 minutes or until spinach wilts. Add cream; bring to a boil, remove from heat.
2 Preheat grill.
3 Remove scallops from shells; rinse and dry shells. Return scallops to shells; grill scallops about 5 minutes or until cooked. Top scallops with spinach mixture then breadcrumbs; grill until browned lightly.
per serving 23g total fat (14.5g saturated fat); 1417kJ (339 cal); 10.4g carbohydrate; 21.8g protein; 3g fibre

poultry

Finger-lickin' delicious when eaten straight off the grill

tamarind, orange and honey drumettes

PREPARATION TIME 15 MINUTES (PLUS REFRIGERATION TIME) COOKING TIME 30 MINUTES SERVES 6

2 teaspoons finely grated orange rind
⅓ cup (80ml) orange juice
⅓ cup (120g) honey
⅓ cup (115g) tamarind concentrate
½ cup (125ml) japanese soy sauce
30 chicken drumettes (2kg)
600g baby buk choy,
  trimmed, quartered
2 medium red capsicums (400g),
  sliced thickly
230g fresh baby corn
1 tablespoon tamarind
  concentrate, extra
2 teaspoons sesame oil

1 Combine rind, juice, honey, tamarind and half the sauce in large bowl, add chicken; turn to coat in marinade. Cover; refrigerate 3 hours or overnight.
2 Cook chicken on heated oiled grill plate, turning and brushing occasionally with marinade, about 30 minutes or until cooked.
3 Meanwhile, cook buk choy, capsicum and corn on heated oiled flat plate until tender. Place vegetables in medium bowl with combined remaining sauce, extra tamarind and oil; toss to combine. Serve with chicken.
per serving 22.3g total fat (6.3g saturated fat); 1994kJ (477 cal); 30.8g carbohydrate; 37g protein; 4.1g fibre

guava-glazed turkey salad with mandarin

PREPARATION TIME 25 MINUTES COOKING TIME 50 MINUTES SERVES 6

⅓ cup (80ml) dry sherry
1 tablespoon golden syrup
1 tablespoon dijon mustard
1 clove garlic, crushed
1 small brown onion (80g),
  chopped finely
⅓ cup (80ml) guava nectar
1.5kg turkey breast fillets
5 medium mandarins (1kg)
300g curly endive, trimmed
⅓ cup coarsely chopped fresh
  flat-leaf parsley

MANDARIN DRESSING
2 tablespoons mandarin juice
1 teaspoon dijon mustard
1 teaspoon white wine vinegar
2 tablespoons guava nectar

1 Combine sherry, syrup, mustard, garlic, onion and nectar in small saucepan; simmer, uncovered, about 10 minutes or until mixture thickens slightly. Stand 5 minutes.
2 Combine sherry mixture in large bowl with turkey. Cook turkey on heated oiled grill plate, turning and brushing occasionally with sherry mixture, about 40 minutes or until cooked. Cover; stand 10 minutes then slice thickly.
3 Meanwhile, segment mandarins over large bowl.
4 Place ingredients for mandarin dressing in screw-top jar; shake well.
5 Combine turkey in bowl with mandarin, endive, parsley and dressing; mix gently.
per serving 8.7g total fat (2g saturated fat); 1672kJ (400 cal); 17.8g carbohydrate; 56.4g protein; 4.1g fibre

burgers italian-style

PREPARATION TIME 20 MINUTES COOKING TIME 30 MINUTES SERVES 4

500g chicken mince
¼ cup (35g) sun-dried tomatoes,
  drained, chopped finely
1 tablespoon finely chopped
  fresh basil
1 egg
1 cup (70g) stale breadcrumbs
3 cloves garlic, crushed
4 slices pancetta (60g)
1 square loaf focaccia (440g)
½ cup (150g) mayonnaise
40g baby rocket leaves
120g bocconcini, sliced thickly

1 Combine chicken in large bowl with tomato, basil, egg, breadcrumbs and about a third of the garlic; shape mixture into four burgers.
2 Cook burgers on heated oiled grill plate about 30 minutes or until cooked.
3 Cook pancetta on grill plate until crisp. Drain.
4 Quarter focaccia; slice each square in half horizontally. Toast cut sides on grill plate.
5 Combine mayonnaise with remaining garlic, spread on focaccia bases; sandwich rocket, burgers, pancetta and cheese between focaccia quarters.
per serving 34.9g total fat (9.3g saturated fat); 3357kJ (803 cal); 71.5g carbohydrate; 47.6g protein; 5.6g fibre

Daikon are large, long, white radishes that have a sweet, fresh flavour without the bite of the common red radish. Used extensively in Japanese cooking, daikon are also great eaten raw in salads, shredded for a garnish, or cooked in stir-fries.

Fontina, a luscious Italian cheese made from cow milk, has a smooth yet firm texture and a mild, nutty flavour. It is ideal for melting or grilling, and is the cheese of choice when making the Italian version of fondue.

sesame wasabi chicken with daikon salad

PREPARATION TIME 20 MINUTES COOKING TIME 40 MINUTES SERVES 4

1 tablespoon japanese soy sauce

1 tablespoon sesame oil

2 tablespoons wasabi paste

8 chicken drumsticks (1.2kg)

DAIKON SALAD

2 medium carrots (240g)

1 small daikon (400g)

6 green onions, sliced thinly

1 tablespoon mirin

1 tablespoon lime juice

2 teaspoons sesame oil

2 teaspoons japanese soy sauce

2 tablespoons roasted sesame seeds

1 Combine sauce, oil and wasabi in large bowl, add chicken; turn to coat in mixture. Cook chicken on heated lightly oiled flat plate, turning and brushing occasionally with marinade, about 40 minutes or until cooked through.

2 Meanwhile, make daikon salad. Serve chicken with salad.

DAIKON SALAD Using vegetable peeler, slice carrots and daikon into ribbons. Place in large bowl with remaining ingredients; toss to combine.

per serving 31.3g total fat (7.7g saturated fat); 1948kJ (466 cal), 7.2g carbohydrate; 36.5g protein; 4.1g fibre

fontina, pancetta and sage chicken

PREPARATION TIME 15 MINUTES COOKING TIME 20 MINUTES SERVES 4

4 x 200g chicken breast fillets

4 thin slices fontina cheese (100g)

4 slices pancetta (60g)

2 tablespoons coarsely chopped fresh sage

2 tablespoons olive oil

2 cloves garlic, crushed

16 whole sage leaves

1 Slit a pocket in one side of each fillet but do not cut all the way through. Divide cheese, pancetta and chopped sage among pockets; secure with toothpicks. Brush chicken with combined oil and garlic.

2 Cook chicken, both sides, on heated oiled grill plate, about 20 minutes or until cooked. Remove toothpicks before serving. Cook whole sage leaves on oiled grill plate until golden brown. Serve chicken topped with sage leaves.

per serving 23.3g total fat (8g saturated fat); 1806kJ (432 cal); 0.3g carbohydrate; 55.3g protein; 0.3g fibre

A quesadilla (from queso, the Spanish word for cheese) is a tortilla folded around a filling of a good-melting shredded cheese and any cooked spiced meat, poultry or bean filling, which is then grilled, fried or toasted and served with salsa. Quesadillas are often sliced into strips before being served as a savoury appetiser or snack.

chicken quesadillas with jalapeño tomato salsa

PREPARATION TIME 20 MINUTES COOKING TIME 15 MINUTES SERVES 4

2 teaspoons mexican chilli powder

2 medium avocados (500g)

¼ cup (60g) sour cream

2 tablespoons lime juice

2 tablespoons vegetable oil

2 teaspoons ground cumin

2 teaspoons ground coriander

1kg chicken tenderloins

8 large flour tortillas (320g)

1 cup (120g) coarsely grated cheddar

JALAPEÑO TOMATO SALSA

4 medium egg tomatoes (300g),
  seeded, chopped finely

¼ cup (60g) bottled jalapeño chillies,
  rinsed, drained, chopped finely

¼ cup coarsely chopped
  fresh coriander

1 medium avocado (250g),
  chopped coarsely

1 tablespoon lime juice

1 Preheat grill.

2 Combine chilli powder, avocados, sour cream and juice in medium bowl; mash roughly with fork.

3 Combine oil and spices in large bowl, add chicken; mix well. Cook chicken in heated oiled grill pan, in batches, until cooked.

4 Meanwhile, combine ingredients for jalapeño tomato salsa in medium bowl.

5 Divide chicken and avocado mixture among tortillas; fold to enclose filling.

6 Place quesadillas on oven tray; sprinkle with cheese. Grill until cheese melts and is golden brown. Serve quesadillas with salsa.

per serving 81g total fat (25.3g saturated fat); 4937kJ (1181 cal); 44.9g carbohydrate; 66.3g protein; 5.5g fibre

An Afro-Portuguese hot sauce made from a fiery small African-grown chilli of the same name, piri piri also contains ginger, garlic, oil and various herbs. It is used for marinating meats or poultry, brushing over grilling foods, or as an ingredient in cooking (splash a little in your next bloody mary).

Sichuan (or szechuan) peppercorns have a natural affinity with duck and there are many classic Chinese dishes that marry the two. Here, the flavours of the snow pea and watercress salad complement the spicy union perfectly.

piri piri quail

PREPARATION TIME 15 MINUTES COOKING TIME 25 MINUTES SERVES 4

6 quails (1kg)
⅓ cup (80ml) piri piri sauce
4 baby eggplants (240g), halved
4 small zucchini (360g), halved
200g yellow grape tomatoes
1 green onion, sliced thinly

CHILLI DRESSING
2 tablespoons piri piri sauce
1 clove garlic
⅓ cup (100g) mayonnaise

1 Combine ingredients for chilli dressing in small bowl.
2 Discard necks from quails. Using scissors, cut along each side of each quail's backbone; discard backbones.
3 Cut quails in half; combine in medium bowl with sauce. Cook quail on heated oiled grill plate about 25 minutes or until cooked.
4 Meanwhile, cook eggplant and zucchini on grill plate until browned both sides. Add tomatoes toward end of vegetables' cooking time; cook, turning, until soft.
5 Serve quail with vegetables and dressing, sprinkled with onion.
per serving 22.3g total fat (4.6g saturated fat); 1442kJ (345 cal); 8.9g carbohydrate; 25.8g protein; 3.8g fibre

sichuan duck with watercress and snow pea salad

PREPARATION TIME 20 MINUTES (PLUS REFRIGERATION TIME) COOKING TIME 40 MINUTES SERVES 4

½ cup (125ml) chinese cooking wine
2 tablespoons light soy sauce
2 cloves garlic, crushed
4cm piece fresh ginger (20g),
  sliced thinly
1 teaspoon sesame oil
4 duck marylands (1.2kg)
2 teaspoons sichuan peppercorns
1 teaspoon sea salt
100g watercress, trimmed
150g snow peas, trimmed,
  sliced thinly
1 small red onion (100g),
  sliced thinly
½ cup loosely packed fresh
  coriander leaves
½ cup (70g) roasted unsalted
  peanuts, chopped coarsely
2 tablespoons lime juice
1 tablespoon peanut oil
1 clove garlic, crushed, extra

1 Combine wine, sauce, garlic, ginger and sesame oil in large bowl with duck. Cover; refrigerate 3 hours or overnight.
2 Drain duck; discard marinade. Dry-fry peppercorns in small frying pan until fragrant. Crush peppercorns and salt using mortar and pestle; press mixture onto duck skin.
3 Cook duck on heated oiled flat plate, turning midway through cooking time, about 40 minutes or until cooked.
4 Meanwhile, combine remaining ingredients in large bowl; serve with duck.
per serving 92.9g total fat (25.6g saturated fat); 4314kJ (1032 cal); 6.5g carbohydrate; 35.1g protein; 4.1g fibre

tikka chicken pizza

PREPARATION TIME 10 MINUTES COOKING TIME 20 MINUTES SERVES 4

2 medium brown onions (300g),
  sliced thinly
1 tablespoon brown sugar
400g chicken tenderloins
¼ cup (75g) tikka paste
⅓ cup (110g) mango chutney
4 pieces naan (200g)
⅓ cup (45g) roasted slivered almonds
⅓ cup (95g) yogurt
⅓ cup (50g) raisins
¼ cup loosely packed fresh
  coriander leaves

1 Combine onion and sugar in small bowl. Cook onion mixture on heated oiled flat plate, turning, about 10 minutes or until mixture caramelises.
2 Meanwhile, slice chicken lengthways into thin strips; combine with paste in medium bowl. Cook chicken on heated oiled grill plate until cooked.
3 Spread chutney over naan; top with onion, chicken and nuts.
4 Cook pizzas on hot grill plate about 5 minutes or until bases are browned lightly. Serve pizzas topped with yogurt, raisins and coriander.
per serving 27.2g total fat (8g saturated fat); 2470kJ (591 cal); 55g carbohydrate; 29.1g protein; 6.2g fibre

cajun spatchcock with spicy tomato salsa

PREPARATION TIME 20 MINUTES COOKING TIME 1 HOUR SERVES 6

6 x 500g spatchcocks
2 tablespoons olive oil
1 small white onion (80g),
  grated coarsely
2 cloves garlic, crushed
2 tablespoons sweet paprika
2 teaspoons ground cinnamon
2 teaspoons ground fennel
2 teaspoons dried oregano

SPICY TOMATO SALSA
6 large egg tomatoes (540g), halved
1 tablespoon olive oil
1 medium brown onion (150g),
  chopped finely
2 cloves garlic, crushed
1 tablespoon sweet paprika
1 teaspoon smoked paprika
1 tablespoon red wine vinegar
1 fresh long red chilli, chopped finely

1 Discard necks from spatchcocks. Using scissors, cut along each side of each spatchcock's backbone; discard backbones. Turn spatchcocks skin-side up; press down on breastbone to flatten.
2 Rub spatchcocks all over with combined remaining ingredients. Cook spatchcocks on heated oiled grill plate, turning midway through cooking time, about 1 hour or until cooked.
3 Meanwhile, make spicy tomato salsa.
4 Serve spatchcocks with spicy tomato salsa.
SPICY TOMATO SALSA Cook tomato on heated oiled grill plate, turning, until softened; chop tomato coarsely. Heat oil in medium saucepan; cook onion and garlic, stirring, until onion softens. Add spices; cook, stirring, until fragrant. Stir in tomato, vinegar and chilli; cook, uncovered, stirring occasionally, about 20 minutes or until salsa thickens.
per serving 48.8g total fat (13.6g saturated fat); 2746kJ (657 cal); 4g carbohydrate; 50.6g protein; 2.1g fibre

indochine grilled chicken salad

PREPARATION TIME 25 MINUTES (PLUS REFRIGERATION TIME) COOKING TIME 40 MINUTES SERVES 4

2 teaspoons five-spice powder
¼ cup (60ml) mirin
2 tablespoons chinese cooking wine
2 cloves garlic, crushed
4 x 200g chicken thigh cutlets
125g rice vermicelli
150g snow peas, sliced thinly
1 cup (80g) bean sprouts
2 green onions, sliced thinly
½ cup coarsely chopped
  fresh coriander
¼ cup loosely packed fresh
  vietnamese mint leaves
2 medium carrots (240g), cut
  into matchsticks

LIME DRESSING
⅓ cup (80ml) lime juice
⅓ cup (80ml) mirin
2 cloves garlic, crushed
1 tablespoon grated palm sugar

1   Combine five-spice, mirin, wine and garlic in large bowl; add chicken, turn to coat in marinade. Cover; refrigerate 3 hours or overnight.
2   Combine ingredients for lime dressing in screw-top jar; shake well.
3   Cook chicken on heated oiled grill plate, turning and brushing occasionally with marinade, about 40 minutes or until cooked.
4   Meanwhile, place vermicelli in large heatproof bowl, cover with boiling water; stand until just tender, drain. Rinse vermicelli under cold water; drain.
5   Place vermicelli and dressing in large bowl with remaining ingredients, toss salad to combine. Serve with chicken.
per serving 20.5g total fat (6.6g saturated fat); 1668kJ (399 cal); 17.2g carbohydrate; 26.9g protein; 4.2g fibre

lemon-chilli butterflied chicken

PREPARATION TIME 25 MINUTES COOKING TIME 55 MINUTES SERVES 4

80g butter, softened
½ teaspoon dried chilli flakes
½ teaspoon cracked black pepper
1 tablespoon finely grated lemon rind
1 tablespoon finely chopped
  fresh rosemary
1.6kg whole chicken
½ cup (35g) stale breadcrumbs
2 teaspoons finely grated lemon
  rind, extra
¼ cup (20g) coarsely
  grated parmesan

1 Move oven shelf to second-bottom position. Preheat grill.
2 Combine butter, chilli, pepper, rind and rosemary in small bowl.
3 Cut along each side of chicken's backbone; discard backbone. Turn chicken skin-side up; press down to flatten. Loosen and lift chicken skin; push butter mixture between skin and flesh.
4 Place chicken, skin-side down, on oiled wire rack in shallow flameproof baking dish. Grill chicken 40 minutes. Turn chicken; cook about 10 minutes or until chicken is cooked.
5 Meanwhile, combine remaining ingredients in small bowl.
6 Remove chicken from dish; strain juices from dish into small heatproof jug. Return chicken to dish; sprinkle with crumb mixture, drizzle ¼ cup (60ml) of the juices over crumb mixture.
7 Grill chicken about 5 minutes or until topping is browned lightly. Quarter chicken; serve with mixed green salad.
per serving 50.5g total fat (21.9g saturated fat); 2705kJ (647 cal); 6g carbohydrate; 43.1g protein; 0.5g fibre

chicken yakitori with sesame dipping sauce

PREPARATION TIME 20 MINUTES COOKING TIME 10 MINUTES SERVES 4

12 chicken tenderloins (1kg)

SESAME DIPPING SAUCE
¼ cup (60ml) light soy sauce
2 tablespoons mirin
3 teaspoons white sugar
½ teaspoon sesame oil
1 teaspoon sesame seeds

1 Combine ingredients for sesame dipping sauce in small saucepan; stir over medium heat until sugar dissolves.
2 Thread each tenderloin onto a skewer; brush skewers with half the dipping sauce. Cook skewers, in batches, in heated oiled grill pan until chicken is cooked. Serve skewers with remaining sesame dipping sauce.
per serving 20.4g total fat (6.4g saturated fat); 1643kJ (393 cal); 3.8g carbohydrate; 47.1g protein; 0.1g fibre

This recipe needs to be cooked in an oven with a grill setting (not under a small grill) or in a covered barbecue by the indirect method.

Yakitori, literally "grilled poultry", is a Japanese staple, and you'll find yakitoriya – barbecue stalls or takeaway shops – scattered throughout the streets of every city, where workers gather for a snack after they leave the office. You need a dozen bamboo skewers for this recipe; soak them in cold water for at least an hour to prevent scorching.

beef

The aroma of a grilling steak carried by the air simply spells summer

mustard-crumbed beef fillet with rocket salad

PREPARATION TIME 20 MINUTES (PLUS REFRIGERATION TIME) COOKING TIME 50 MINUTES (PLUS STANDING TIME) SERVES 6

¼ cup (70g) prepared horseradish
1 tablespoon olive oil
1kg piece beef eye-fillet
2 tablespoons wholegrain mustard
1 tablespoon coarsely chopped
  fresh flat-leaf parsley
½ cup (35g) fresh breadcrumbs
1 tablespoon butter, melted

ROCKET SALAD
100g baby rocket leaves
1 medium red onion (170g),
  sliced thinly
8 green onions, sliced thinly
¼ cup (40g) roasted pine nuts
⅓ cup (80ml) balsamic vinegar
⅓ cup (80ml) olive oil

1 Combine horseradish and oil in large bowl; add beef, turn to coat in mixture. Cover; refrigerate 3 hours or overnight.
2 Cook beef in heated oiled grill pan, turning, until browned all over. Reduce heat; cook beef, turning occasionally, about 30 minutes or until cooked. Cover, stand 10 minutes.
3 Meanwhile, combine ingredients for rocket salad in large bowl.
4 Preheat grill.
5 Combine mustard, parsley and breadcrumbs in small bowl with half the butter. Brush beef with remaining butter; press breadcrumb mixture over beef. Grill beef until crust is browned. Stand 10 minutes; slice thickly. Serve beef with rocket salad.
per serving 34.2g total fat (9.1g saturated fat); 2082kJ (498 cal); 8.7g carbohydrate; 38.4g protein; 1.9g fibre

For this recipe, make certain that you use prepared white horseradish and not bottled horseradish cream.

FLAVOURED

BUTTERS

chilli, lemon and parsley

mustard and tarragon

caper and anchovy

dill and gherkin

sumac

pickled ginger

wasabi

roasted capsicum and olive

chilli, lemon and parsley

PREPARATION TIME 5 MINUTES (PLUS FREEZING TIME) SERVES 6

Combine 80g softened butter, ½ teaspoon dried chilli flakes, 2 teaspoons finely grated lemon rind and 2 tablespoons finely chopped fresh flat-leaf parsley in small bowl. Place on piece of plastic wrap; shape into 6cm log, wrap tightly. Freeze until firm; remove 15 minutes before serving.

per tablespoon 16.4g total fat (10.8g saturated fat); 615kJ (147 cal); 0.2g carbohydrate; 0.2g protein; 0.2g fibre

mustard and tarragon

PREPARATION TIME 5 MINUTES (PLUS FREEZING TIME) SERVES 6

Combine 80g softened butter, 2 teaspoons wholegrain mustard and 2 teaspoons finely chopped fresh tarragon in small bowl. Place on piece of plastic wrap; shape into 6cm log, wrap tightly. Freeze until firm; remove 15 minutes before serving.

per tablespoon 16.4g total fat (10.8g saturated fat); 614kJ (147 cal); 0.2g carbohydrate; 0.2g protein; 0.1g fibre

caper and anchovy

PREPARATION TIME 5 MINUTES (PLUS FREEZING TIME) SERVES 6

Finely chop 1 tablespoon drained rinsed capers; combine in small bowl with 80g softened butter and 2 drained coarsely chopped anchovy fillets. Place on piece of plastic wrap; shape into 6cm log, wrap tightly. Freeze until firm; remove 15 minutes before serving.

per tablespoon 16.6g total fat (10.8g saturated fat); 631kJ (151 cal); 0.5g carbohydrate; 0.6g protein; 0.1g fibre

dill and gherkin

PREPARATION TIME 5 MINUTES (PLUS FREEZING TIME) SERVES 6

Combine 80g softened butter, 2 tablespoons finely chopped gherkin, 2 tablespoons finely chopped fresh dill and ½ teaspoon cracked black pepper in small bowl. Place on piece of plastic wrap; shape into 6cm log, wrap tightly. Freeze until firm; remove 15 minutes before serving.

per tablespoon 16.4g total fat (10.8g saturated fat); 631kJ (151 cal); 1.4g carbohydrate; 0.2g protein; 0.2g fibre

sumac

PREPARATION TIME 5 MINUTES (PLUS FREEZING TIME) SERVES 6

Combine 80g softened butter and 1 tablespoon sumac in small bowl. Place on piece of plastic wrap; shape into 6cm log, wrap tightly. Freeze until firm; remove 15 minutes before serving.

per tablespoon 16.4g total fat (10.8g saturated fat); 610kJ (146 cal); 0.1g carbohydrate; 0.1g protein; 0g fibre

pickled ginger

PREPARATION TIME 5 MINUTES (PLUS FREEZING TIME) SERVES 6

Combine 80g softened butter and 2 tablespoons finely chopped pickled pink ginger in small bowl. Place on piece of plastic wrap; shape into 6cm log, wrap tightly. Freeze until firm; remove 15 minutes before serving.

per tablespoon 16.4g total fat (10.8g saturated fat); 619kJ (148 cal); 0.4g carbohydrate; 0.2g protein; 0.2g fibre

wasabi

PREPARATION TIME 5 MINUTES (PLUS FREEZING TIME) SERVES 6

Combine 80g softened butter, 2 teaspoons wasabi paste and 1 finely chopped green onion in small bowl. Place on piece of plastic wrap; shape into 6cm log, wrap tightly. Freeze until firm; remove 15 minutes before serving.

per tablespoon 16.4g total fat (10.8g saturated fat); 610kJ (146 cal); 0.1g carbohydrate; 0.1g protein; 0g fibre

roasted capsicum and olive

PREPARATION TIME 5 MINUTES (PLUS FREEZING TIME) SERVES 6

Finely chop 1 tablespoon seeded black olives; combine in small bowl with 80g softened butter, 1 tablespoon finely chopped roasted red capsicum and 1 tablespoon finely chopped fresh oregano. Place on piece of plastic wrap; shape into 6cm log, wrap tightly. Freeze until firm; remove 15 minutes before serving.

per tablespoon 16.4g total fat (10.8g saturated fat); 610kJ (146 cal); 0.7g carbohydrate; 0.1g protein; 0.1g fibre

veal parmigiana

PREPARATION TIME 25 MINUTES COOKING TIME 25 MINUTES SERVES 4

2 teaspoons olive oil

2 teaspoons lemon juice

1 clove garlic, crushed

1 small eggplant (230g)

4 x 100g veal schnitzels

¼ cup (35g) plain flour

⅔ cup (170g) bottled tomato pasta
sauce, warmed

120g bocconcini, sliced thinly

4 slices char-grilled capsicum (100g),
drained, sliced thinly

1 medium tomato (150g), seeded,
chopped finely

1 tablespoon coarsely chopped
fresh basil

¼ cup (20g) shaved parmesan

1 tablespoon fresh basil leaves

1 Combine oil, juice and garlic in small bowl. Cut eggplant lengthways into six slices; discard the two skin-side pieces, brush remaining eggplant, both sides, with oil mixture. Cook eggplant, both sides, in heated grill pan until tender.

2 Meanwhile, coat veal in flour; shake off excess. Cook veal in oiled grill pan until cooked.

3 Preheat grill.

4 Place veal on oiled oven tray; top each piece with pasta sauce, eggplant and bocconcini. Grill until bocconcini melts.

5 Meanwhile, combine capsicum, tomato, chopped basil and parmesan in small bowl. Divide mixture among veal pieces; grill until parmesan melts. Sprinkle parmigiana with basil leaves; serve with a mixed green leaf salad.

per serving 12.3g total fat (5g saturated fat); 1250kJ (299 cal); 13.4g carbohydrate; 32.1g protein; 2.8g fibre

spiced sliced rump with chilli peanut sauce

PREPARATION TIME 30 MINUTES COOKING TIME 15 MINUTES SERVES 4

1 fresh small red thai chilli,
chopped finely

1 shallot (25g), chopped finely

1 tablespoon peanut oil

800g beef rump steak

¼ cup (60ml) water

⅓ cup (75g) caster sugar

¼ cup (60ml) fish sauce

½ cup (125ml) lime juice

1 medium carrot (120g),
chopped finely

1 medium red capsicum (200g),
chopped finely

1 cup (140g) crushed roasted
unsalted peanuts

20 peking duck pancakes (200g)

1 Combine chilli and shallot in medium bowl. Combine half the chilli mixture with oil in large bowl; add beef, turn to coat in mixture.

2 Cook beef on heated oiled flat plate, turning once, until cooked. Cover; stand 5 minutes, slice thinly.

3 Meanwhile, stir the water, sugar, sauce, juice, carrot, capsicum and nuts into remaining chilli mixture.

4 Heat pancakes by folding each into quarters; place in steamer over large saucepan of simmering water until just pliable. Serve beef with chilli peanut sauce and pancakes.

per serving 35.6g total fat (9.4g saturated fat); 3047kJ (729 cal); 41.1g carbohydrate; 58.6g protein; 5.4g fibre

Peking duck pancakes are small, crepe-like pancakes sold fresh, usually in containers holding 20, located in the refrigerated section of most Asian grocery stores. Steam them for just a few minutes, until they are warm and pliable.

Lentils have a nutty, earthy flavour that helps ground the strident richness of the sausages and pungency of the mustard and spices in this robust salad.

char-grilled T-bones with potato pancakes

PREPARATION TIME 20 MINUTES COOKING TIME 30 MINUTES SERVES 4

3 fresh long red chillies,
  chopped finely
2cm piece fresh ginger (10g), grated
2 cloves garlic, crushed
2 tablespoons olive oil
4 x 300g beef T-bone steaks
4 trimmed corn cobs (1kg)
4 medium potatoes (800g),
  grated coarsely
50g butter

1 Combine chilli, ginger, garlic and oil in large bowl; add steaks, turn to coat in mixture. Cook steaks on heated oiled grill plate. Cover; stand 5 minutes.

2 Meanwhile, cook corn, turning occasionally, on flat plate until tender.

3 To make potato pancakes, squeeze excess moisture from potato; divide into four portions. Heat half the butter on flat plate; cook potato portions, flattening with spatula, until browned both sides.

4 Spread corn with remaining butter; serve with steaks and potato pancakes.

per serving 33.1g total fat (13g saturated fat); 3118kJ (746 cal); 53.4g carbohydrate; 52.8g protein; 11.4g fibre

beef sausage and lentil salad

PREPARATION TIME 30 MINUTES COOKING TIME 40 MINUTES SERVES 4

2 cups (400g) brown lentils
2 sprigs fresh thyme
20 baby beetroots (500g), trimmed
8 thick beef sausages (1.2kg)
2 teaspoons olive oil
1 large brown onion (200g),
  chopped finely
2 teaspoons yellow mustard seeds
2 teaspoons ground cumin
1 teaspoon ground coriander
½ cup (125ml) chicken stock
100g baby spinach leaves

THYME DRESSING
1 teaspoon fresh thyme leaves
1 clove garlic, crushed
½ cup (125ml) red wine vinegar
¼ cup (60ml) olive oil

1 Place ingredients for thyme dressing in screw-top jar; shake well.

2 Cook lentils in large saucepan of boiling water with thyme until lentils are tender; drain, discard thyme. Combine lentils in large bowl with half the dressing.

3 Meanwhile, boil, steam or microwave unpeeled beetroots until tender; drain. When cool enough to handle, peel and halve beetroots.

4 Cook sausages in heated oiled grill pan until cooked. Stand 5 minutes, slice thickly.

5 Heat oil in small saucepan; cook onion, seeds and spices, stirring, until onion softens. Add stock; bring to a boil.

6 Combine onion mixture, spinach, beetroot, sausage and remaining dressing in bowl with lentils.

per serving 94.5g total fat (39.2g saturated fat); 5676kJ (1358 cal); 55.8g carbohydrate; 62.8g protein; 26.4g fibre

Pasilla (pronounced pah-SEE-yah) chillies, also called "chile negro" because of their dark brown colour, are the wrinkled, dried version of fresh chilaca chillies. About 20cm in length, a pasilla is only mildly hot, but possesses a rich flavour that adds smoky depth to the overall recipe.

mexican-spiced grilled rump with chilli beans

PREPARATION TIME 25 MINUTES (PLUS STANDING TIME) COOKING TIME 1 HOUR 20 MINUTES SERVES 4

2 cups (400g) dried black beans
2 pasilla chillies (10g)
¼ cup (60ml) boiling water
2 tablespoons olive oil
1 medium brown onion (150g),
  chopped finely
3 cloves garlic, crushed
¼ cup (70g) tomato paste
4 medium tomatoes (600g),
  chopped coarsely
½ cup (125ml) water
2 tablespoons lime juice
2 tablespoons brown sugar
1 tablespoon dried marjoram
2 teaspoons smoked paprika
1kg beef rump steak
8 large flour tortillas (320g)
1 small iceberg lettuce,
  trimmed, shredded
⅔ cup (160g) sour cream
1 small red onion (100g),
  sliced thinly
⅓ cup firmly packed fresh
  coriander leaves

1   Place beans in large bowl of cold water, cover with water; stand overnight. Rinse under cold water; drain. Cook beans in large saucepan of boiling water, uncovered, until tender; drain. Rinse under cold water; drain.
2   Meanwhile, soak chillies in the boiling water in a small bowl 20 minutes; blend or process mixture until smooth.
3   Heat half the oil in large saucepan; cook brown onion and garlic, stirring, until onion softens. Add chilli mixture, paste, tomato, the water, juice and sugar; bring to a boil. Remove from heat; blend or process until smooth.
4   Return chilli mixture to pan; add beans, simmer, covered, 20 minutes. Uncover; simmer about 10 minutes or until sauce thickens.
5   Meanwhile, combine marjoram, paprika and remaining oil in large bowl; add beef, turn to coat in mixture. Cook beef, both sides, on heated oiled grill plate until cooked. Cover; stand 10 minutes, slice thinly.
6   Divide tortillas into two batches; wrap each batch in a double thickness of foil. Heat tortilla parcels, turning occasionally, on grill plate about 5 minutes or until warm. Serve tortillas with chilli beans, beef, lettuce, sour cream, red onion and coriander.
per serving 49.8g total fat (20.4g saturated fat); 5158kJ (1234 cal); 96.2g carbohydrate; 92g protein; 21.4g fibre

cantonese beef patties with grilled gai lan

PREPARATION TIME 30 MINUTES COOKING TIME 15 MINUTES SERVES 4

800g beef mince

1 medium brown onion (150g),
  chopped finely

3 cloves garlic, crushed

2cm piece fresh ginger (10g), grated

1 fresh small red thai chilli,
  chopped finely

227g can water chestnuts, drained,
  rinsed, chopped finely

¼ cup finely chopped fresh chives

1 egg

½ cup (35g) fresh breadcrumbs

1 tablespoon hoisin sauce

1 tablespoon water

2 tablespoons oyster sauce

⅓ cup (80ml) hoisin sauce, extra

2 teaspoons sesame oil

1kg gai lan, chopped coarsely

1 Combine beef, onion, two-thirds of the garlic, ginger, chilli, chestnuts, chives, egg, breadcrumbs and hoisin sauce in large bowl; shape mixture into eight patties.

2 Combine the water, oyster sauce, extra hoisin sauce and remaining garlic in small bowl. Reserve ¼ cup (60ml) hoisin mixture.

3 Brush patties with remaining hoisin mixture; cook patties, both sides, in heated oiled grill pan about 10 minutes or until cooked.

4 Heat sesame oil in same grill pan; cook gai lan until wilted. Serve gai lan topped with patties, drizzled with reserved hoisin mixture.

per serving 20.2g total fat (6.8g saturated fat); 2077kJ (497 cal); 26.6g carbohydrate; 48g protein; 8.3g fibre

ultimate steak sandwich

PREPARATION TIME 20 MINUTES COOKING TIME 40 MINUTES SERVES 4

2 tablespoons vegetable oil

2 large red onions (600g),
  sliced thinly

1 tablespoon brown sugar

2 tablespoons balsamic vinegar

200g swiss brown mushrooms,
  sliced thinly

4 x 200g beef scotch fillet steaks

8 thick slices ciabatta (360g)

100g pâté

¼ cup (70g) wholegrain mustard

40g baby rocket leaves

1 Heat half the oil on flat plate; cook onion, turning constantly, until browned lightly. Sprinkle onion with sugar and vinegar; cook, turning constantly, until onion is caramelised. Transfer onion to small bowl; cover to keep warm.

2 Heat remaining oil on flat plate; cook mushrooms, turning, until browned and tender.

3 Meanwhile, cook steaks on flat plate until cooked. Cover; stand while toasting bread, both sides, on flat plate.

4 Sandwich pâté, mustard, rocket, mushrooms, steak and onion between bread slices.

per serving 32.8g total fat (8.9g saturated fat); 4025kJ (963 cal); 92.2g carbohydrate; 67.7g protein; 15.2g fibre

Hoisin is a sweet, thick chinese barbecue sauce made from salted fermented soy beans, onion and garlic. Used as a marinade or baste, or as a flavouring for stir-fried, braised or roasted foods, it can be found in all Asian food shops and most supermarkets.

We used a simple port and chicken-liver pâté in our sandwich, but you can use whatever type of pâté you like best.

79

American mustard,
flavoured with sugar
and vinegar or white
wine, is bright yellow
and very mild in flavour.

barbecued scotch fillet

PREPARATION TIME 10 MINUTES (PLUS REFRIGERATION TIME) COOKING TIME 1 HOUR 30 MINUTES (PLUS STANDING TIME) SERVES 6

¼ cup (60ml) barbecue sauce
2 tablespoons american mustard
4 cloves garlic, crushed
½ cup (125ml) beer
1.4kg piece beef scotch fillet

1 Combine sauce, mustard, garlic and beer in large bowl; add beef, turn to coat in mixture. Cover; refrigerate 3 hours or overnight.
2 Place beef and marinade in lightly oiled disposable aluminium baking dish. Cook, covered, using indirect heat, about 1½ hours or until cooked as desired. Cover; stand 15 minutes, slice thinly.
per serving 14.2g total fat (5.9g saturated fat); 1488kJ (356 cal); 5.9g carbohydrate; 49.7g protein; 0.6g fibre

veal chops with grilled fennel and mandarin

PREPARATION TIME 25 MINUTES COOKING TIME 20 MINUTES SERVES 4

4 x 200g veal chops
2 baby fennel bulbs (260g), trimmed,
  halved lengthways
4 small mandarins (400g), peeled,
  halved horizontally

SALSA VERDE
¼ cup finely chopped fresh
  flat-leaf parsley
¼ cup finely chopped fresh mint
1 tablespoon finely chopped
  fennel tips
¼ cup finely chopped fresh chives
1 tablespoon wholegrain mustard
2 tablespoons lemon juice
2 tablespoons drained baby capers,
  rinsed, chopped finely
1 clove garlic, crushed
⅓ cup (80ml) olive oil

1 Cook veal on heated oiled grill plate until cooked. Cook fennel and mandarin on grill plate until just browned.
2 Combine ingredients for salsa verde in small bowl.
3 Serve veal, fennel and mandarin topped with salsa verde.
per serving 21.6g total fat (3.5g saturated fat); 1492kJ (357 cal); 8.4g carbohydrate; 30.4g protein; 3.3g fibre

Za'atar, a blend of roasted dry herbs and spices such as thyme, wild oregano, sumac, cumin and paprika, is easy to make, but a prepared mixture can be purchased in all Middle Eastern food shops and some delicatessens. Keep what you don't use on these chops stored, in a glass jar with a tight-fitting lid, in the fridge for future use.

za'atar-spiced veal loin chops with fattoush

PREPARATION TIME 15 MINUTES COOKING TIME 20 MINUTES SERVES 4

4 x 200g veal loin chops

ZA'ATAR
1 tablespoon sumac
1 tablespoon roasted sesame seeds
2 teaspoons finely chopped
  fresh thyme
1 tablespoon olive oil
1 teaspoon dried marjoram

FATTOUSH
2 large pitta breads (160g)
4 medium tomatoes (600g), cut
  into wedges
2 lebanese cucumbers (260g),
  seeded, sliced thinly
1 medium green capsicum (200g),
  cut into 2cm pieces
3 green onions, sliced thinly
1 cup coarsely chopped fresh
  flat-leaf parsley
½ cup coarsely chopped fresh mint
½ cup (125ml) olive oil
¼ cup (60ml) lemon juice
2 cloves garlic, crushed

1 Preheat grill.
2 Combine ingredients for za'atar in small bowl.
3 Make fattoush.
4 Grill veal until browned both sides and cooked. Sprinkle about a tablespoon of the za'atar equally over the veal; serve with fattoush.

FATTOUSH Grill bread until crisp; break into small pieces. Combine tomato, cucumber, capsicum, onion and herbs in large bowl. Just before serving, toss bread and combined oil, juice and garlic into salad.

per serving 38.9g total fat (5.9g saturated fat); 2587kJ (619 cal); 27.8g carbohydrate; 36.5g protein; 17.1g fibre

Calves liver should be cut into paper-thin slices then quickly seared because too much cooking will destroy its soft, delicate texture. Your butcher will slice the liver thinly for you.

seared calves liver with caramelised onion

PREPARATION TIME 15 MINUTES COOKING TIME 30 MINUTES SERVES 4

5 small red onions (500g),
 sliced thinly
1 tablespoon brown sugar
1½ tablespoons balsamic vinegar
3 medium potatoes (600g), unpeeled,
 cut into 1cm slices
1 tablespoon olive oil
600g calves liver, sliced thinly

1 Cook onion on heated oiled flat plate, turning constantly, until browned lightly. Sprinkle onion with sugar and vinegar; cook, turning constantly, until onion is caramelised. Transfer onion to small bowl; cover to keep warm.
2 Meanwhile, boil, steam or microwave potato until tender; drain, combine in large bowl with oil. Cook potato on heated oiled grill plate until browned.
3 Meanwhile, cook liver on grill plate until browned both sides and just cooked. Serve liver with onion and potato.
per serving 13.1g total fat (3.3g saturated fat); 1660kJ (397 cal); 34.2g carbohydrate; 33g protein; 4g fibre

grilled meatballs and penne

PREPARATION TIME 30 MINUTES COOKING TIME 45 MINUTES SERVES 6

600g beef mince
1 cup (100g) packaged breadcrumbs
¼ cup finely chopped fresh
 flat-leaf parsley
¼ cup (20g) finely grated parmesan
2 eggs
1 tablespoon olive oil
1 medium white onion (150g),
 chopped finely
1 clove garlic, crushed
700g bottled tomato pasta sauce
400g can diced tomatoes
½ cup (125ml) chicken stock
¼ cup firmly packed fresh basil leaves
500g penne
2 cups (200g) coarsely grated mozzarella

1 Combine beef, breadcrumbs, parsley, parmesan and eggs in medium bowl. Roll level tablespoons of mixture into balls; flatten slightly.
2 Cook meatballs in heated oiled grill pan until browned all over.
3 Heat oil in deep 3-litre (12-cup) flameproof baking dish. Cook onion and garlic until onion softens. Add sauce, undrained tomatoes, stock and basil; bring to a boil.
4 Add meatballs to sauce; simmer, covered with foil, about 20 minutes or until meatballs are cooked, stirring occasionally.
5 Cook pasta in large saucepan of boiling water until just tender; drain.
6 Preheat grill.
7 Combine pasta with meatballs and sauce, sprinkle with mozzarella; grill until cheese melts and is browned lightly.
per serving 22.7g total fat (9.7g saturated fat); 3081kJ (737 cal); 82.6g carbohydrate; 46.9g protein; 6.8g fibre

chilli-rubbed hickory-smoked rib-eye steaks

PREPARATION TIME 10 MINUTES (PLUS REFRIGERATION AND STANDING TIME) COOKING TIME 10 MINUTES SERVES 4

1 tablespoon finely grated lemon rind

2 teaspoons chilli powder

2 teaspoons dried thyme

1 teaspoon sweet smoked paprika

2 tablespoons olive oil

2 cloves garlic, crushed

4 x 200g beef rib-eye steaks

100g hickory smoking chips

2 cups (500ml) water

1 Combine rind, chilli, thyme, paprika, oil and garlic in large bowl with steaks. Cover; refrigerate 3 hours or overnight.

2 Soak chips in the water in medium bowl; stand 3 hours or overnight.

3 Place drained chips in smoke box alongside steaks on grill plate. Cook steaks, covered, using indirect heat, about 10 minutes or until cooked.

per serving 27.3g total fat (8.9g saturated fat); 1726kJ (413 cal); 0.4g carbohydrate; 41.1g protein; 0.7g fibre

cheese-stuffed steaks with radicchio salad

PREPARATION TIME 20 MINUTES COOKING TIME 20 MINUTES SERVES 4

4 x 125g beef eye-fillet steaks

80g brie, sliced thickly into 4 pieces

1 small radicchio (150g), trimmed, quartered

1 cup (120g) roasted pecans, chopped coarsely

1 large pear (330g), unpeeled, sliced thickly

1 cup loosely packed fresh flat-leaf parsley

¼ cup (60ml) olive oil

2 tablespoons lemon juice

1 Slice steaks in half horizontally. Sandwich cheese slices between steak halves; tie with kitchen string to secure.

2 Cook steaks on heated oiled grill plate until cooked.

3 Meanwhile, cook radicchio on grill plate until browned lightly.

4 Combine radicchio with remaining ingredients in bowl; serve with steaks.

per serving 48.1g total fat (9.8g saturated fat); 2596kJ (621 cal); 12g carbohydrate; 34.2g protein; 5.4g fibre

The hickory smoking chips called for here are available at most barbecue supply stores, as are other varieties of wood chips that can also be used to smoke meat on the barbecue.

We used a triple-cream brie cheese here; you can replace it with the more easily found blue-vein variety, if you prefer, but choose one that's mild and very creamy.

lamb

Souvlaki, kebob, shashlik, brochette: the whole world grills lamb

merguez with parmesan polenta triangles

PREPARATION TIME 25 MINUTES (PLUS REFRIGERATION TIME) COOKING TIME 35 MINUTES SERVES 4

1 litre (4 cups) water
1 cup (170g) polenta
20g cold butter, chopped
1 cup (80g) finely grated parmesan
8 merguez sausages (640g)

SUMMER SALAD
1 small red onion (100g),
 chopped finely
4 green onions, sliced thinly
1 lebanese cucumber (130g),
 seeded, chopped finely
1 trimmed celery stalk (100g),
 sliced thinly
1 medium yellow capsicum (200g),
 chopped finely
½ cup loosely packed fresh
 flat-leaf parsley
½ cup loosely packed fresh
 mint leaves
2 teaspoons finely grated lemon rind
2 tablespoons lemon juice
2 tablespoons olive oil
1 tablespoon white wine vinegar

1 Oil deep 19cm-square cake pan.
2 Place the water in large saucepan; bring to a boil. Gradually stir polenta into water; simmer, stirring, about 10 minutes or until polenta thickens, stir in butter and cheese. Spread polenta into pan; cool 10 minutes. Cover; refrigerate 3 hours or until firm.
3 Meanwhile, make summer salad.
4 Turn polenta onto board. Cut polenta into four squares; cut squares into triangles. Cook polenta, both sides, in heated oiled grill pan until browned and hot. Cover to keep warm.
5 Cook sausages in same grill pan until cooked. Serve with salad and polenta.
SUMMER SALAD Combine onions, cucumber, celery, capsicum and herbs in large bowl. Drizzle with combined rind, juice, oil and vinegar; toss gently.
per serving 66.8g total fat (25.7g saturated fat); 3975kJ (951 cal); 38.3g carbohydrate; 44g protein; 4.4g fibre

A spicy sausage that originated in Tunisia, merguez has become traditional fare throughout North Africa and Spain. Made with lamb and identified by its uncooked chilli-red colour, fried or grilled merguez is as often added to a tagine as it is eaten atop a mound of fruity couscous.

Rogan josh is a rich, aromatic curry from the north of India that is recognisable by its wonderful depth of flavour rather than spiciness. The curry paste of the same name is available from most supermarkets; adjust the amount you use to suit your palate.

lamb stack with capsicum, eggplant and pesto

PREPARATION TIME 20 MINUTES COOKING TIME 25 MINUTES SERVES 4

¼ cup (20g) finely grated parmesan
¼ cup (40g) roasted pine nuts
1 clove garlic, quartered
½ cup (125ml) olive oil
1 cup firmly packed fresh basil leaves
1 tablespoon lemon juice
2 medium red capsicums (400g)
1 small eggplant (230g), cut into
  8 slices crossways
4 lamb backstraps (800g)

1 To make pesto, blend or process cheese, nuts and garlic with half the oil until combined. Add basil and remaining oil; blend until pesto forms a smooth, thick puree. Stir in juice.

2 Quarter capsicums; discard seeds and membranes. Roast under grill or in very hot oven, skin-side up, until skin blisters and blackens. Cover capsicum pieces with plastic or paper for 5 minutes; peel away skin.

3 Cook eggplant on heated oiled grill plate until tender.

4 Cook lamb, in batches, on grill plate until cooked. Cover, stand 5 minutes, slice thickly.

5 Make four stacks, on serving plates, from eggplant, lamb and capsicum; spoon pesto over each stack.

per serving 55.1g total fat (13.5g saturated fat); 2959kJ (708 cal); 5.7g carbohydrate; 47.3g protein; 3.5g fibre

loin chops rogan josh with pulao salad

PREPARATION TIME 10 MINUTES COOKING TIME 20 MINUTES SERVES 6

12 lamb loin chops (1.2kg)
½ cup (150g) rogan josh curry paste
1½ cups (300g) basmati rice
¼ teaspoon ground turmeric
1 cardamom pod, bruised
⅓ cup (45g) roasted slivered almonds
⅓ cup (55g) sultanas
⅓ cup firmly packed fresh
  coriander leaves
⅓ cup coarsely chopped fresh mint

MUSTARD SEED DRESSING
¼ cup (60ml) olive oil
2 tablespoons yellow mustard seeds
¼ cup (60ml) white wine vinegar
1 tablespoon white sugar

1 Combine lamb and paste in large bowl; turn lamb to coat in paste.

2 Make mustard seed dressing.

3 Cook rice, turmeric and cardamom in large saucepan of boiling water until rice is tender; drain.

4 Meanwhile, cook lamb, in batches, in heated oiled grill pan until cooked.

5 To make pulao salad, combine rice in large bowl with nuts, sultanas, herbs and dressing. Serve pulao salad with lamb.

MUSTARD SEED DRESSING Heat oil in small saucepan; cook seeds, stirring constantly, over low heat, until aromatic and softened. Place seeds, vinegar and sugar in screw-top jar; shake well.

per serving 41.6g total fat (11.6g saturated fat); 3072kJ (735 cal); 51.7g carbohydrate; 37.2g protein; 4.2g fibre

lemon and garlic kebabs with greek salad

PREPARATION TIME 25 MINUTES COOKING TIME 5 MINUTES SERVES 4

8 x 15cm stalks fresh rosemary

800g lamb fillets, diced into
  3cm pieces

3 cloves garlic, crushed

2 tablespoons olive oil

2 teaspoons finely grated lemon rind

1 tablespoon lemon juice

GREEK SALAD

5 medium egg tomatoes (375g),
  cut into wedges

2 lebanese cucumbers (260g),
  halved lengthways, sliced thinly

1 medium red capsicum (200g),
  diced into 2cm pieces

1 medium green capsicum (200g),
  diced into 2cm pieces

1 medium red onion (170g),
  sliced thinly

¼ cup (40g) seeded kalamata olives

200g fetta cheese, diced into
  2cm pieces

2 teaspoons fresh oregano leaves

¼ cup (60ml) olive oil

2 tablespoons cider vinegar

1 Remove leaves from bottom two-thirds of each rosemary stalk; sharpen trimmed ends to a point.

2 Thread lamb onto rosemary skewers. Brush kebabs with combined garlic, oil, rind and juice. Cover; refrigerate until required.

3 Combine ingredients for greek salad in large bowl; toss gently.

4 Cook kebabs on heated oiled grill plate, brushing frequently with remaining garlic mixture, until cooked. Serve kebabs with greek salad.

per serving 52.5g total fat (18.9g saturated fat); 3085kJ (738 cal); 11.2g carbohydrate; 54.1g protein; 4.1g fibre

Gözleme (pronounced goz-LEH-meh), from Anatolia in Turkey, is a centuries-old village dish made of flat bread folded around various ingredients then cooked on a grill or griddle. Traditionally, gözleme, being an economical peasant dish, contains less meat filling than does ours.

gözleme

PREPARATION TIME 50 MINUTES COOKING TIME 40 MINUTES SERVES 6

4 cups (600g) plain flour

1 teaspoon coarse cooking salt

1²⁄₃ cups (410ml) warm water

2 tablespoons vegetable oil

LAMB FILLING

1 tablespoon vegetable oil

2 teaspoons ground cumin

½ teaspoon hot paprika

3 cloves garlic, crushed

500g lamb mince

400g can diced tomatoes

½ cup coarsely chopped fresh
  flat-leaf parsley

SPINACH AND CHEESE FILLING

300g spinach, trimmed,
  shredded finely

½ cup coarsely chopped fresh mint

1 small brown onion (80g),
  chopped finely

½ teaspoon ground allspice

250g fetta, crumbled

1 cup (100g) coarsely grated mozzarella

1 Combine flour and salt in large bowl. Gradually stir in the water; mix to a soft dough. Knead dough on floured surface about 5 minutes or until smooth and elastic. Return to bowl; cover.

2 Make lamb filling.

3 Combine ingredients for spinach and cheese filling in medium bowl.

4 Divide dough into six pieces; roll each piece into 30cm square. Divide spinach and cheese filling among dough squares, spreading filling across centre of squares; top each with equal amounts of lamb filling. Fold top and bottom edges of dough over filling; tuck in ends to enclose.

5 Cook gözleme, both sides, over low heat on oiled grill plate, brushing with oil, until browned lightly and heated through.

LAMB FILLING Heat oil in large frying pan; cook spices and garlic until fragrant. Add lamb; cook, stirring, until browned. Add undrained tomatoes; simmer about 15 minutes or until liquid is almost evaporated. Stir in parsley.

per serving 29.9g total fat (12.7g saturated fat); 3168kJ (758 cal); 75.8g carbohydrate; 41.8g protein, 7.1g fibre

lemon grass lamb with vietnamese vermicelli salad

PREPARATION TIME 25 MINUTES COOKING TIME 20 MINUTES SERVES 4

10cm stick (20g) fresh lemon grass,
  chopped finely
2 tablespoons light soy sauce
1 tablespoon brown sugar
2 tablespoons vegetable oil
3 lamb backstraps (600g)
70g rice vermicelli
2 lebanese cucumbers (260g),
  seeded, sliced thinly
½ small pineapple (450g),
  chopped coarsely
1 cup (80g) bean sprouts
1 cup loosely packed fresh
  coriander leaves
1 cup loosely packed fresh
  mint leaves
1 large carrot (180g), grated coarsely
1 large butter lettuce, trimmed,
  leaves separated

CHILLI LIME DRESSING
¼ cup (60ml) hot water
2 tablespoons fish sauce
1 tablespoon brown sugar
2 tablespoons lime juice
2 fresh small red thai chillies,
  chopped finely
1 clove garlic, crushed

1 Combine ingredients for chilli lime dressing in screw-top jar; shake well.
2 Combine lemon grass, sauce, sugar and oil in medium bowl; add lamb, turn to coat in mixture.
3 Place vermicelli in medium heatproof bowl; cover with boiling water. Stand until just tender; drain. Rinse under cold water; drain.
4 Combine vermicelli in large bowl with cucumber, pineapple, sprouts, herbs, carrot and 2 tablespoons of the dressing; toss gently.
5 Cook lamb, both sides, on heated oiled grill plate until cooked. Cover; stand 5 minutes, slice thinly.
6 Top lettuce with salad; serve with lamb, drizzled with remaining dressing.
per serving 22.9g total fat (7.2g saturated fat); 1856kJ (444 cal); 20.6g carbohydrate; 35.9g protein; 6g fibre

moroccan-spiced lamb leg with fruity couscous

PREPARATION TIME 25 MINUTES (PLUS REFRIGERATION TIME) COOKING TIME 35 MINUTES (PLUS STANDING TIME) SERVES 6

2 tablespoons ras el hanout

2 tablespoons olive oil

1.5kg butterflied lamb leg

FRUITY COUSCOUS

1½ cups (375ml) water

1½ cups (300g) couscous

2 medium oranges (480g)

1 cup (230g) fresh dates,
  seeded, quartered

1 cup (100g) roasted walnuts,
  chopped coarsely

⅓ cup coarsely chopped fresh
  flat-leaf parsley

½ cup (125ml) orange juice

2 tablespoons walnut oil

½ teaspoon ground cinnamon

1 Combine ras el hanout and oil in large bowl, add lamb; turn to coat in marinade. Cover; refrigerate 3 hours or overnight.

2 Meanwhile, make fruity couscous.

3 Cook lamb on heated oiled grill plate, covered, about 35 minutes or until cooked, turning midway through cooking. Cover; stand 10 minutes, slice thickly. Serve lamb with couscous.

FRUITY COUSCOUS Place the water in medium saucepan; bring to a boil, remove from heat. Stir in couscous. Cover; stand about 5 minutes or until liquid is absorbed, fluffing occasionally with fork. Segment oranges over pan. Add remaining ingredients; mix gently.

per serving 37.6g total fat (8.1g saturated fat); 3490kJ (835 cal); 57.4g carbohydrate; 65.2g protein; 4.6g fibre

dukkah-crusted cutlets with roasted garlic yogurt

PREPARATION TIME 10 MINUTES COOKING TIME 20 MINUTES SERVES 4

6 cloves garlic, unpeeled

1 teaspoon vegetable oil

1 cup (280g) yogurt

2 tablespoons roasted hazelnuts

2 tablespoons roasted pistachios

2 tablespoons sesame seeds

2 tablespoons ground coriander

1 tablespoon ground cumin

12 french-trimmed lamb cutlets (600g)

1 Preheat oven to moderate (180°C/160°C fan-forced).

2 Place garlic on oven tray; drizzle with oil. Roast 10 minutes. Peel garlic then crush in small bowl with yogurt. Cover; refrigerate.

3 To make dukkah, blend or process nuts until chopped finely. Dry-fry seeds and spices in small frying pan until fragrant; combine with nuts in medium bowl, add lamb, turn to coat in dukkah mixture.

4 Cook lamb, both sides, in heated oiled grill pan until cooked. Serve lamb with roasted garlic yogurt.

per serving 27.8g total fat (8.7g saturated fat); 1547kJ (370 cal); 5.7g carbohydrate; 22.9g protein; 2.9g fibre

With a name that loosely translates as "top of the shop", ras el hanout is a Moroccan blend of the best a spice merchant has to offer: allspice, cumin, paprika, fennel, caraway and saffron are all generally part of the mix. Stir a little into steamed couscous to add colour and aroma. It is available from Middle Eastern and specialty spice stores.

An Egyptian blend of nuts, spices and seeds, dukkah is used as a dip when mixed with oil or into mayonnaise, or sprinkled over meats, salads or vegetables as a flavour-enhancer. If you don't want to make this recipe, dukkah is available, ready-made, from delicatessens and specialty spice shops.

99

pork

Grilling pork presents the meat at its succulent best

roasted peppered pork

PREPARATION TIME 10 MINUTES COOKING TIME 1 HOUR 30 MINUTES SERVES 6

1 tablespoon coarse cooking salt

1 tablespoon green peppercorns, crushed

1 tablespoon pink peppercorns, crushed

1 tablespoon white peppercorns, crushed

1 tablespoon black peppercorns, crushed

1kg piece pork shoulder

cooking-oil spray

1 Combine salt and peppercorns in small bowl.

2 Score rind of pork, spray pork with oil. Rub pepper mixture over pork.

3 Cook pork in disposable aluminium baking dish, covered, using indirect heat, about 1½ hours or until cooked.

4 Cover pork; stand 10 minutes, slice thickly.

per serving 19.2g total fat (7.3g saturated fat); 1371kJ (328 cal); 0g carbohydrate; 39g protein; 0g fibre

GRILLED
FRUIT

sweet lime mangoes

figs with mascarpone

chocolaty bananas

pineapple with passionfruit

brandied pears

caramelised peaches

almond crumble nectarines

plums with fresh honeycomb

sweet lime mangoes

PREPARATION TIME 5 MINUTES COOKING TIME 8 MINUTES SERVES 4

Preheat grill. Slice cheeks from 4 mangoes; score each in shallow criss-cross pattern. Combine 1 tablespoon grated lime rind and 1 tablespoon lime juice; drizzle over each cheek, sprinkle each with 1 teaspoon brown sugar. Grill until sugar caramelises; serve with ½ cup yogurt.

per serving 1.7g total fat (0.7g saturated fat); 798kJ (191 cal); 35.8g carbohydrate; 4.1g protein; 4.1g fibre

figs with mascarpone

PREPARATION TIME 10 MINUTES COOKING TIME 5 MINUTES SERVES 4

Preheat grill. Combine 1 cup (250g) mascarpone with 2 tablespoons ricotta in bowl; beat until smooth, stir in 2 tablespoons honey. Combine 1 tablespoon sugar and ½ teaspoon ground cinnamon in bowl. Halve 8 fresh figs. Dip cut surface into sugar mixture; place on oven tray, cut-side up. Grill until brown; serve with mascarpone.

per serving 31.3g total fat (21.1g saturated fat); 1806kJ (432 cal); 31.6g carbohydrate; 6.3g protein; 4g fibre

chocolaty bananas

PREPARATION TIME 5 MINUTES COOKING TIME 30 MINUTES SERVES 4

Cut 12cm-long slit in 4 unpeeled bananas; place bananas on pieces of foil. Chop 150g dark eating chocolate coarsely; divide among slits. Drizzle 2 tablespoons rum into slits; wrap bananas in foil. Cook on heated grill plate about 30 minutes or until skins blacken. Serve with whipped cream, if desired.

per serving 11.6g total fat (10.4g saturated fat); 1639kJ (392 cal); 61.2g carbohydrate; 4.9g protein; 6.1g fibre

pineapple with passionfruit

PREPARATION TIME 10 MINUTES COOKING TIME 12 MINUTES SERVES 4

Toast ¼ cup flaked coconut in heated grill pan until browned lightly. Halve a small pineapple lengthways; peel and core one half; cut lengthways into 12 pieces (reserve remaining half for another use). Brown pineapple both sides in heated grill pan. Top with combined 2 tablespoons Malibu liqueur and ⅓ cup passionfruit pulp; sprinkle with coconut.

per serving 3.3g total fat (2.8g saturated fat); 481kJ (115 cal); 10.8g carbohydrate; 2.1g protein; 5.9g fibre

brandied pears

PREPARATION TIME 5 MINUTES COOKING TIME 8 MINUTES SERVES 4

Preheat grill. Halve 4 pears lengthways; place halves on greased oven tray. Top with 2 tablespoons brandy; sprinkle with 2 tablespoons caster sugar. Grill until golden brown. Serve with vanilla ice-cream, if desired.

per serving 0.2g total fat (0g saturated fat); 748kJ (179 cal); 37.4g carbohydrate; 0.7g protein; 5.3g fibre

caramelised peaches

PREPARATION TIME 5 MINUTES COOKING TIME 8 MINUTES SERVES 4

Combine 1 cup yogurt with ¼ teaspoon ground cinnamon and ¼ teaspoon ground cardamom in bowl. Halve 4 peaches. Cook peach halves, cut-side down, on heated oiled grill plate until browned; turn. Sprinkle 2 tablespoons brown sugar over cut sides; turn, cook until sugar bubbles. Serve peaches with spiced yogurt.

per serving 2.3g total fat (1.4g saturated fat); 481kJ (115 cal); 17.5g carbohydrate; 4.2g protein; 1.8g fibre

almond crumble nectarines

PREPARATION TIME 10 MINUTES COOKING TIME 15 MINUTES SERVES 4

Halve 4 nectarines. Combine 2 tablespoons plain flour, ¼ teaspoon ground cinnamon, 1 tablespoon brown sugar, ¼ cup muesli and 2 tablespoons flaked almonds in bowl with 1 tablespoon softened butter. Spoon mixture into hollows in nectarines; place, filling-side up, in baking dish. Pour ½ cup sweet dessert wine into dish, cover; cook on heated grill plate about 15 minutes.

per serving 8g total fat (3g saturated fat); 794kJ (190 cal); 23g carbohydrate; 4.1g protein; 5.1g fibre

plums with fresh honeycomb

PREPARATION TIME 10 MINUTES COOKING TIME 7 MINUTES SERVES 4

Combine ¼ cup sugar, ¼ cup water and 1 tablespoon Madeira in pan; stir over heat until sugar dissolves. Boil gently until syrup is thickened slightly. Halve 8 plums. Brush cut sides with syrup; place, cut-sides down, on heated oiled grill plate. Cook about 1 minute or until softened. Serve plums with remaining syrup; top with 40g coarsely chopped fresh honeycomb.

per serving 0.2g total fat (0g saturated fat); 702kJ (168 cal); 35.9g carbohydrate; 0.9g protein; 3.3g fibre

mexican pork cutlets with avocado salsa

PREPARATION TIME 10 MINUTES COOKING TIME 10 MINUTES SERVES 4

2 tablespoons taco seasoning mix

¼ cup (60ml) olive oil

4 x 235g pork cutlets

3 small tomatoes (270g),
  seeded, chopped finely

1 small avocado (200g),
  chopped finely

1 lebanese cucumber (130g),
  seeded, chopped finely

1 tablespoon lime juice

1 Combine seasoning, 2 tablespoons of the oil and pork in large bowl. Cook pork on heated oiled grill plate until cooked.

2 Meanwhile, combine remaining oil in medium bowl with tomato, avocado, cucumber and juice. Serve pork with salsa.

per serving 42.2g total fat (10.7g saturated fat); 2241kJ (536 cal); 1.2g carbohydrate; 38g protein; 1.2g fibre

grilled loin chops with apple and onion plum sauce

PREPARATION TIME 10 MINUTES COOKING TIME 20 MINUTES SERVES 4

2 medium apples (300g)

1 tablespoon olive oil

1 medium red onion (170g),
  cut into thin wedges

4 x 280g pork loin chops

½ cup (125ml) plum sauce

¼ cup (60ml) lemon juice

⅓ cup (80ml) chicken stock

1 Cut each unpeeled, uncored apple horizontally into four slices. Heat oil in grill pan; cook apple and onion, turning, until softened.

2 Meanwhile, cook pork on heated oiled grill plate until cooked.

3 Stir sauce, juice and stock into apple mixture; simmer 1 minute. Serve pork with sauce.

per serving 29.7g total fat (9.1g saturated fat); 2404kJ (575 cal); 32g carbohydrate; 45g protein; 1.8g fibre

Found in most supermarkets, sachets of taco seasoning mix are meant to duplicate the taste of a Mexican sauce made from cumin, oregano, chillies and other spices.

You can buy bottled teriyaki sauce at any supermarket, but it's very easy to make yourself – all you need is soy sauce, cooking sake, mirin and sugar. 'I'he key ingredient is the mirin, which gives both a lovely aroma and lustre to a dish: teriyaki actually translates as lustrous (teri) grilled (yaki) food.

We used a good-quality egg mayonnaise and ready-made fried shallots in assembling this burger. The shallots, available packaged in most Asian food stores, will keep for months if stored tightly sealed.

teriyaki pork with pineapple

PREPARATION TIME 20 MINUTES (PLUS REFRIGERATION TIME) COOKING TIME 20 MINUTES SERVES 4

⅓ cup (80ml) mirin
¼ cup (60ml) japanese soy sauce
2 tablespoons cooking sake
2 teaspoons white sugar
5cm piece fresh ginger (25g), grated
2 cloves garlic, crushed
600g pork fillets
1 small pineapple (900g),
  sliced thinly
2 green onions, sliced thinly

1 Combine mirin, sauce, sake, sugar, ginger and garlic in large bowl; add pork, turn to coat in marinade. Cover; refrigerate 3 hours or overnight.
2 Drain pork; reserve marinade. Cook pork on heated oiled grill plate until browned and cooked as desired. Cover; stand 10 minutes.
3 Cook pineapple on grill plate about 2 minutes or until soft.
4 Bring reserved marinade to a boil in small saucepan; cook about 5 minutes or until sauce reduces by half.
5 Serve sliced pork with pineapple and onion; drizzle with sauce.
per serving 12.2g total fat (4.1g saturated fat); 1371kJ (328 cal); 13.3g carbohydrate; 34.1g protein; 3g fibre

chilli pork burger

PREPARATION TIME 15 MINUTES COOKING TIME 20 MINUTES SERVES 4

700g pork mince
1 small red onion (100g),
  chopped finely
⅓ cup coarsely chopped
  fresh coriander
¼ cup (15g) stale breadcrumbs
1 egg
1 fresh long red chilli, chopped finely
4 hamburger buns (360g)
⅓ cup (100g) mayonnaise
50g mizuna
⅓ cup (25g) fried shallots

CARAMELISED CAPSICUM SALSA
1 medium red capsicum (200g),
  sliced thinly
1 large red onion (300g), sliced thinly
½ cup (125ml) sweet chilli sauce

1 Combine pork in large bowl with onion, coriander, breadcrumbs, egg and chilli; shape mixture into four patties.
2 Cook patties on heated oiled grill plate until cooked through.
3 Meanwhile, make caramelised capsicum salsa.
4 Split buns in half; toast cut sides. Spread mayonnaise on bun bases; sandwich mizuna, patties, salsa and shallots between bun halves.
CARAMELISED CAPSICUM SALSA Cook capsicum and onion on heated oiled flat plate until onion softens. Add sauce; cook, turning gently, about 2 minutes or until mixture caramelises.
per serving 26.6g total fat (6.6g saturated fat); 3018kJ (722 cal); 68.6g carbohydrate; 48.1g protein; 7.2g fibre

barbecued spareribs with red cabbage coleslaw

PREPARATION TIME 15 MINUTES (PLUS REFRIGERATION TIME) COOKING TIME 25 MINUTES SERVES 4

**2kg slabs american-style
pork spareribs**

BARBECUE SAUCE
1 cup (250ml) tomato sauce
¾ cup (180ml) cider vinegar
2 tablespoons olive oil
¼ cup (60ml) worcestershire sauce
**⅓ cup (75g) firmly packed
brown sugar**
2 tablespoons american mustard
1 teaspoon cracked black pepper
**2 fresh small red thai chillies,
finely chopped**
2 cloves garlic, crushed
2 tablespoons lemon juice

RED CABBAGE COLESLAW
½ cup (120g) sour cream
¼ cup (60ml) lemon juice
2 tablespoons water
**½ small red cabbage (600g),
shredded finely**
3 green onions, sliced thinly

1 Make barbecue sauce.
2 Place ribs in large shallow baking dish. Pour sauce over ribs, cover; refrigerate 3 hours or overnight, turning ribs occasionally.
3 Make red cabbage coleslaw.
4 Drain ribs; reserve sauce. Cook ribs on heated oiled grill plate, brushing occasionally with reserved sauce, about 15 minutes or until cooked. Turn ribs midway through cooking time.
5 Bring remaining sauce to a boil in small saucepan; cook about 4 minutes or until sauce thickens slightly.
6 Cut ribs into serving-sized pieces; serve with hot barbecue sauce and red cabbage coleslaw.
BARBECUE SAUCE Combine ingredients in medium saucepan; bring to a boil. Cool 10 minutes.
RED CABBAGE COLESLAW Combine sour cream, juice and the water in screw-top jar; shake well. Combine dressing in large bowl with cabbage and onion. Cover; refrigerate until required.
per serving 39.9g total fat (15.2g saturated fat); 3210kJ (768 cal); 44.4g carbohydrate; 53.6g protein; 8g fibre

barbecued pork neck with five-spice star-anise glaze

PREPARATION TIME 15 MINUTES COOKING TIME 1 HOUR 20 MINUTES (PLUS STANDING TIME) SERVES 6

1kg piece pork neck

1 clove garlic, sliced thinly

4cm piece ginger (20g), sliced thinly

2 x 100g packets baby asian greens

FIVE-SPICE STAR-ANISE GLAZE

1¼ cups (310ml) water

1 cup (220g) firmly packed
  brown sugar

3 fresh long red chillies,
  chopped finely

1 star anise

1 teaspoon five-spice powder

⅓ cup (80ml) light soy sauce

¼ cup (60ml) rice vinegar

1 Make five-spice star-anise glaze. Reserve 1 cup (250ml) of glaze.

2 Make several shallow cuts in pork. Press garlic and ginger into cuts; brush ¼ cup (60ml) of the remaining glaze over pork.

3 Cook pork on heated oiled flat plate, covered, over low heat, 30 minutes. Turn pork; cook, covered, 30 minutes. Increase heat to high; cook, uncovered, 5 minutes, turning and brushing with remaining glaze constantly. Remove pork from heat. Cover; stand 15 minutes, slice thickly.

4 Meanwhile, place reserved glaze in small saucepan; simmer about 5 minutes or until thickened slightly. Cool.

5 Combine greens with glaze in medium bowl; serve with pork.

FIVE-SPICE STAR-ANISE GLAZE Combine the water and sugar in medium saucepan; simmer about 10 minutes or until glaze thickens slightly. Remove from heat; stir in remaining ingredients.

per serving 13.4g total fat (4.5g saturated fat); 1714kJ (410 cal), 36.4g carbohydrate; 36.5g protein; 0.6g fibre

mixed grill with warm potato salad

PREPARATION TIME 25 MINUTES COOKING TIME 45 MINUTES SERVES 4

700g kipfler potatoes,
  halved lengthways

1 tablespoon olive oil

2 cloves garlic, crushed

2 teaspoons caraway seeds

½ small cabbage (600g),
  shredded coarsely

4 pork butterflied steaks (400g)

4 thick pork sausages (480g)

4 thin bacon rashers (120g),
  rind removed

⅓ cup (80ml) olive oil, extra

¼ cup (60ml) white wine vinegar

2 teaspoons dijon mustard

1 Preheat oven to hot (220°C/200°C fan-forced).

2 Combine potato, oil, garlic and seeds in large shallow baking dish. Roast about 30 minutes or until potato is browned lightly.

3 Remove potato mixture from oven; stir in cabbage. Return to oven; cook, uncovered, about 15 minutes or until cabbage wilts.

4 Meanwhile, cook steaks, sausages and bacon, in batches, on heated oiled grill plate. Remove from heat; cover to keep warm.

5 Combine extra oil, vinegar and mustard in large bowl with potato mixture. Serve mixed grill with warm salad.

per serving 61g total fat (17.9g saturated fat); 2724kJ (891 cal); 31.2g carbohydrate; 49.7g protein; 10.1g fibre

The use of the word "jerk" in culinary terms refers to a spicy jamaican seasoning used to marinate meat, seafood or poultry before grilling or roasting it. While each cook has his or her particular favourite combination of spices, jerk almost always contains allspice, thyme and chilli. Piri piri, an Afro-Portuguese hot sauce, is made from a tiny red chilli of the same name, ground with ginger, garlic, oil and various herbs. It can be used in a marinade or as an ingredient, but is most often applied as a glaze, brushed constantly over meat or poultry as it's being grilled.

jerk pork cutlets with pumpkin chips

PREPARATION TIME 15 MINUTES COOKING TIME 25 MINUTES SERVES 4

3 long green chillies,
  chopped coarsely
3 green onions, chopped coarsely
2 cloves garlic, crushed
1 teaspoon ground allspice
1 teaspoon dried thyme
1 teaspoon white sugar
1 tablespoon light soy sauce
1 tablespoon lime juice
4 x 280g pork loin chops
1kg piece pumpkin, trimmed
2 tablespoons vegetable oil

PIRI PIRI DIPPING SAUCE
⅓ cup (100g) mayonnaise
2 tablespoons piri piri sauce

1 Combine chilli, onion, garlic, allspice, thyme, sugar, sauce, juice and pork in medium bowl.
2 Combine ingredients for piri piri dipping sauce in small bowl.
3 Cut pumpkin into 7cm chips; boil, steam or microwave until tender. Drain; combine chips with oil in medium bowl. Cook chips on heated oiled grill plate until browned.
4 Meanwhile, cook pork on grill plate until cooked. Serve pork with chips and dipping sauce.
per serving 39g total fat (9.8g saturated fat); 2554kJ (611 cal); 21.6g carbohydrate; 42.1g protein; 3.6g fibre

glossary

ALLSPICE also known as pimento or jamaican pepper; so-named because it tastes like a combination of nutmeg, cumin, clove and cinnamon – all spices. Available whole or ground.

ALMONDS flat, pointy-ended nuts with a pitted brown shell enclosing a creamy white kernel covered by a brown skin. There are two types; sweet and bitter.
blanched brown skins removed.
flaked paper-thin slices.
slivered small lengthways-cut pieces.

AMERICAN-STYLE PORK SPARERIBS trimmed, long mid-loin pork ribs; sold in racks of eight or 10 ribs.

BACON RASHERS also known as slices of bacon.

BARBECUE SAUCE a spicy, tomato-based sauce.

BALMAIN BUG a type of crayfish closely related to the lobster.

BASIL an aromatic herb; there are many types, but the most commonly used is sweet basil.

BEETROOT also known as red beet.

BICARBONATE OF SODA also known as baking soda.

BITTERS also known as Angostura bitters; produced from rum infused with herbs and spices.

BLACK BEANS also known as turtle beans; are not the same as chinese black beans, which are fermented soy beans. Available from health food stores and many food outlets.

BREAD
ciabatta means "slipper" in Italian, which is the traditional shape of this popular crisp-crusted white bread.
focaccia an Italian flat bread; similar to thick pizza, usually made with a dimpled surface that is drizzled with olive oil and sprinkled with salt before baking.
naan round leavened bread associated with tandoori dishes of northern India where it is baked pressed against the inside wall of a heated clay oven.
tortilla thin, round unleavened bread originating in Mexico. Two kinds are available, one made from wheat flour and the other from corn (maize).

turkish also known as pide. Comes in long (about 45cm) flat loaves as well as individual rounds; made from wheat flour and sprinkled with sesame or black onion seeds.
pitta also known as lebanese bread. Sold as large flat pieces that separate into two thin rounds, or as small thick pieces called *pocket pitta*.

BREADCRUMBS
packaged fine-textured, crunchy, purchased white breadcrumbs.
stale one- or two-day-old bread made into crumbs by grating, blending or processing.

BROAD BEANS also known as fava, windsor and horse beans; available dried, fresh, canned and frozen. Fresh and frozen are best peeled twice (discarding the beige-green tough inner shell).

BROCCOLINI a cross between broccoli and chinese kale, is milder and sweeter than broccoli; from floret to stem, broccolini is completely edible.

BUK CHOY also called bok choy, bak choy, pak choy and chinese white cabbage; has a fresh, mild mustard taste. *Baby buk choy* is smaller and more tender than buk choy.

BUTTER use salted or unsalted (sweet) butter; 125g is equal to one stick of butter.

CAPERS the grey-green buds of a warm climate (usually Mediterranean) shrub; sold either dried and salted or pickled in a vinegar brine. *Baby capers* are fuller-flavoured than the full-grown ones. Rinse well before use.

CAPSICUM also known as bell pepper or, simply, pepper. Discard seeds and membranes before use. Also available char-grilled in jars from supermarkets.

CARAWAY SEEDS a member of the parsley family; available in seed or ground form and appropriate for sweet and savoury dishes.

CARDAMOM native to India, this spice can be purchased in pod, seed or ground form.

CAYENNE PEPPER a thin-fleshed, long, extremely hot red chilli usually sold dried and ground.

CHEESE
blue mould-treated cheese mottled with blue veining.
bocconcini walnut-sized baby mozzarella; a delicate, semi-soft, white cheese. Spoils rapidly so must be kept under refrigeration in brine for one or two days at most.
cheddar a semi-hard cow-milk cheese. It ranges in colour from white to pale yellow and has a slightly crumbly texture if properly matured.
fetta a crumbly goat- or sheep-milk cheese with a sharp salty taste.
fontina a smooth firm cheese with a nutty taste and a brown or red rind.
haloumi a firm, cream-coloured sheep-milk cheese, somewhat like a minty, salty fetta in flavour; haloumi can be grilled or fried, briefly, without breaking down.
mascarpone a fresh, unripened, smooth, triple-cream cheese with a rich, sweet, slightly acidic taste.
mozzarella a soft, spun-curd cheese. Has a low melting point and an elastic texture when heated, and is used to add texture rather than flavour.
parmesan a hard, grainy cow-milk cheese also known as parmigiano.
ricotta a low-fat, fresh unripened cheese made from whey.

CHICKPEAS also called garbanzos, channa or hummus; round, sandy-coloured legume.

CHILLIES generally the smaller the chilli, the hotter it is. Use rubber gloves when seeding and chopping fresh chillies to prevent burning your skin.
flakes dried, deep-red, dehydrated chilli slices and whole seeds.
jalapeño fairly hot green chillies, available bottled in brine or fresh from specialty greengrocers.
pasilla medium-hot, smoky dried chilli; replace with a mild chilli powder.
red thai small, very hot and bright red; can be substituted with fresh serrano or habanero chillies.

CHINESE COOKING WINE a clear distillation of fermented rice, water and salt; used in marinades and sauces.

CHIVES related to the onion and leek; has a subtle onion flavour.

CHORIZO a sausage of Spanish origin, made of coarsely ground pork and highly seasoned with garlic and chillies.

CINNAMON dried inner bark of the shoots of the cinnamon tree; available in stick or ground form. Cinnamon sticks are available from major spice shops and supermarkets.

COOKING SAKE also known as japanese cooking rice wine and ryori shu. Made from alcohol, rice, salt and corn syrup; often used in marinades.

CORIANDER also known as cilantro or chinese parsley; bright-green leafy herb with a pungent flavour. Also sold as seeds, whole or ground.

COUSCOUS a fine, grain-like cereal product made from semolina; originally from North Africa.

CUCUMBER, LEBANESE short, slender and thin-skinned; tender, edible skin with a sweet, fresh taste.

CURLY ENDIVE also known as frisée; a curly-leafed green salad vegetable.

CURRY
paste some recipes in this book call for commercially prepared pastes of varying strengths and flavours. Use whichever one you feel suits your spice-level tolerance best.
powder a blend of ground spices used for convenience when making curries; available as mild or hot.
tikka a mild paste; consists of chilli, coriander, cumin, lentil flour, garlic, ginger, oil, turmeric, fennel, pepper, cloves, cinnamon and cardamom.

DAIKON also known as giant white radish; has a sweet, fresh flavour without the bite of the more common red radish.

DRUMETTE small, fleshy section of a chicken wing between the shoulder and "elbow"; the meat is scraped down the bone to make a "handle".

EGG some recipes call for raw or barely cooked eggs; exercise caution if there's a salmonella problem in your area.

EGGPLANT purple-skinned vegetable also known as aubergine. Can also be purchased char-grilled, packed in oil, in jars.

FENNEL also known as finocchio or anis; a crisp, pale-green vegetable. Also the name given to its dried seeds, which have a licorice flavour.

FISH SAUCE also called nam pla or nuoc nam; made from pulverised salted fermented fish, most often anchovies. Has a pungent smell and strong taste; use sparingly.

FIVE-SPICE POWDER fragrant ground mixture of cinnamon, clove, star anise, sichuan pepper and fennel seeds. Also known as chinese five-spice.

FLOUR, PLAIN an all-purpose flour made from wheat.

GAI LAN also known as chinese kale, gai lum and chinese broccoli; prized more for its stems than coarse leaves.

GINGER
fresh also known as root ginger; the thick gnarled root of a tropical plant.
pickled pink pickled paper-thin shavings of ginger in a mixture of vinegar, sugar and natural colouring. Available from Asian grocery stores.

GOLDEN SYRUP a by-product of refined sugarcane; pure maple syrup or honey can be substituted.

GUAVA NECTAR a sweet, musky juice made from the pulp of the tropical guava fruit, water and sugar.

HOISIN SAUCE a thick, sweet chinese barbecue sauce made from salted fermented soy beans, onion and garlic.

HONEYCOMB, FRESH the edible chewy structure made of beeswax that houses the honey; available from specialty food and health food stores.

HUMMUS dip made from chickpeas, garlic, lemon juice and tahini (sesame seed paste); can be purchased from most delicatessens and supermarkets.

KAFFIR LIME LEAVES aromatic leaves of a citrus tree; looks like two glossy dark green leaves joined end to end, forming a rounded hourglass shape. A strip of fresh lime peel may be substituted for each kaffir lime leaf.

KALAMATA OLIVES sharp-tasting, small black olives that have been cured in a red-wine brine.

KECAP MANIS a thick soy sauce with added sugar and spices.

KUMARA orange-fleshed sweet potato, often confused with yam.

LEMON GRASS a tall, lemon-smelling and -tasting grass; the white lower part of the stem is used.

LENTILS dried pulses often identified by and named after their colour.

LETTUCE
butter have small, round, loosely formed heads with soft, buttery-textured leaves. Has a sweet flavour.
iceberg a heavy, firm round lettuce with tightly packed leaves and a crisp texture.
radicchio burgundy leaves with white ribs and a slightly bitter flavour.

LIME PICKLE mixed pickle condiment of limes that adds a hot, spicy taste to meals; use sparingly. Available from Indian food stores

MANDARIN also known as tangerine.

MARYLAND poultry leg and thigh still connected in a single piece, with bones and skin intact.

MESCLUN a salad mixture of assorted young lettuce and other green leaves.

MINCE also known as ground meat, as in beef, veal, pork, lamb and chicken.

MIRIN a sweetened rice wine used in Japanese cooking; not to be confused with sake.

MIZUNA frizzy green salad leaf having a delicate mustard flavour.

MUSHROOMS
button small, cultivated white mushrooms with a mild flavour.
enoki clumps of long, spaghetti-like stems with tiny, snowy white caps.
flat large and flat with a rich earthy flavour; ideal for filling and barbecuing.
oyster also known as abalone; grey-white mushroom shaped like a fan. Prized for their smooth texture and subtle, oyster-like flavour.
shiitake when fresh are also known as chinese black, forest or golden oak mushrooms; large and meaty with the earthiness and taste of wild mushrooms.
swiss brown light to dark brown with full-bodied flavour; also known as roman or cremini.

MUSTARD

american flavoured with sugar and vinegar or white wine; is bright yellow and very mild in flavour.

dijon a pale brown, distinctively flavoured fairly mild french mustard.

seeds available in black, brown or yellow varieties. Available from major supermarkets or health food stores.

wholegrain also known as seeded mustard; a coarse-grain mustard made from black and yellow mustard seeds and dijon-style mustard.

NORI a type of dried seaweed used in Japanese cooking. Sold toasted or plain, in thin sheets or shredded.

ONIONS

green also known as scallion or, incorrectly, shallot; an immature onion picked before the bulb has formed.

red also known as spanish, red spanish or bermuda onion; a large, sweet-flavoured, purple-red onion.

OYSTER SAUCE made from oysters and their brine, cooked with salt and soy sauce then thickened. *"Vegetarian" oyster sauce* is available, made from blended mushrooms and soy sauce.

PALM SUGAR also known as jaggery, made from the sap of the sugar palm tree. Creamy to brown in colour, usually sold in rock-hard cakes; if unavailable substitute it with brown sugar.

PANCETTA Italian unsmoked cured pork belly; bacon can be substituted.

PAPRIKA ground dried red capsicum (bell pepper); available smoked, sweet or hot.

PARSLEY, FLAT-LEAF also known as continental or italian parsley.

PENNE translated literally as "quills"; ridged pasta cut into short lengths.

PINE NUTS also known as pignoli; not, in fact, a nut, but a small, cream-coloured kernel from pine cones.

POLENTA also known as cornmeal; a flour-like cereal made of dried, ground corn (maize). Also the name of the dish using it as the main ingredient.

POTATOES

coliban round with smooth white skin and flesh. Good for baking and mashing.

desiree oval, smooth and pink-skinned, with a waxy yellow flesh; good in salads, boiled and roasted.

king edward slightly plump and rosy; great mashed.

kipfler finger-shaped potato with a nutty flavour. Good roasted and in salads.

russet burbank also known as idaho; russet in colour, fabulous baked.

sebago oval and white skinned; good fried, mashed and baked.

PRAWNS also known as shrimp.

PRESERVED LEMON a North African specialty, the citrus is preserved in a mixture of salt and lemon juice. Only the rind is used; rinsed and eaten as is, or added to casseroles and tagines to impart a rich salty-sour acidic flavour.

PROSCIUTTO cured, air-dried, pressed ham; usually sold thinly sliced.

QUAIL domestically grown game birds ranging in weight from 250g to 300g; also known as partridge.

RAISINS dried sweet grapes.

RICE VERMICELLI also known as sen mee, mei fun or bee hoon. Used throughout Asia in spring rolls.

RISONI also known as orzo; a small, rice-shaped pasta used often in soups.

ROCKET also known as arugula, rugula and rucola; a peppery-tasting green leaf. *Baby rocket leaves* are both smaller and less peppery.

SAVOY CABBAGE large, heavy head with crinkled dark-green outer leaves; a fairly mild-tasting cabbage.

SEAFOOD some recipes in this book call for raw or uncooked fish and other seafood; exercise caution if there's a salmonella problem in your area.

SHALLOTS also called french shallots, golden shallots or eschalots; small, brown-skinned, elongated members of the onion family.

fried also known as homm jiew; available in jars or cellophane bags from Asian grocery stores. Once opened, they keep for months if kept tightly sealed. You can make your own by frying thinly sliced peeled shallots until golden-brown and crisp.

SPATCHCOCK a small chicken (poussin), no more than six weeks old, weighing a maximum 500g. Also, a cooking technique where poultry is split open then flattened and grilled.

SPINACH also known as english spinach and, incorrectly, silver beet.

STAR ANISE a dried, star-shaped pod whose seeds have an astringent aniseed flavour.

SULTANAS dried grapes, also known as golden raisins.

SUMAC a purple-red, astringent spice that adds a tart, lemony flavour; goes well with barbecued meats. Can be found in Middle-Eastern food stores.

TAMARILLO also known as tree tomato. Has a black or orange flesh that surrounds a nest of seeds. Is more acidic than sweet.

TAMARIND CONCENTRATE the commercial distillation of tamarind pulp into a condensed paste. Used straight from the container, with no soaking or straining required.

TOFU also known as bean curd, made from the "milk" of crushed soy beans; comes fresh as soft or firm, and processed as fried or pressed dried sheets. *Silken tofu* refers to the method of straining the soy liquid through silk.

TURMERIC, GROUND also known as kamin; known for the golden colour it imparts to dishes.

VEAL SCHNITZEL thinly sliced steak available crumbed or plain; we used plain schnitzel in our recipes.

VIETNAMESE MINT narrow-leafed, pungent herb; also known as cambodian mint and laksa leaf.

WASABI an asian horseradish used for the pungent, green-coloured sauce served with Japanese raw fish dishes; available in powder or paste form.

ZA'ATAR a dry blend of roasted sesame seeds, wild marjoram, thyme and sumac. Available from Middle Eastern food shops.

ZUCCHINI also known as courgette.

index

conversion chart

MEASURES

One Australian metric measuring cup holds approximately 250ml; one Australian metric tablespoon holds 20ml; one Australian metric teaspoon holds 5ml.

The difference between one country's measuring cups and another's is within a two- or three-teaspoon variance, and will not affect your cooking results. North America, New Zealand and the United Kingdom use a 15ml tablespoon.

All cup and spoon measurements are level. The most accurate way of measuring dry ingredients is to weigh them. When measuring liquids, use a clear glass or plastic jug with the metric markings.

We use large eggs with an average weight of 60g.

DRY MEASURES

METRIC	IMPERIAL
15g	½oz
30g	1oz
60g	2oz
90g	3oz
125g	4oz (¼lb)
155g	5oz
185g	6oz
220g	7oz
250g	8oz (½lb)
280g	9oz
315g	10oz
345g	11oz
375g	12oz (¾lb)
410g	13oz
440g	14oz
470g	15oz
500g	16oz (1lb)
750g	24oz (1½lb)
1kg	32oz (2lb)

LIQUID MEASURES

METRIC	IMPERIAL
30ml	1 fluid oz
60ml	2 fluid oz
100ml	3 fluid oz
125ml	4 fluid oz
150ml	5 fluid oz (¼ pint/1 gill)
190ml	6 fluid oz
250ml	8 fluid oz
300ml	10 fluid oz (½ pint)
500ml	16 fluid oz
600ml	20 fluid oz (1 pint)
1000ml (1 litre)	1¾ pints

LENGTH MEASURES

METRIC	IMPERIAL
3mm	⅛in
6mm	¼in
1cm	½in
2cm	¾in
2.5cm	1in
5cm	2in
6cm	2½in
8cm	3in
10cm	4in
13cm	5in
15cm	6in
18cm	7in
20cm	8in
23cm	9in
25cm	10in
28cm	11in
30cm	12in (1ft)

OVEN TEMPERATURES

These oven temperatures are only a guide for conventional ovens. For fan-forced ovens, check the manufacturer's manual.

	°C (CELSIUS)	°F (FAHRENHEIT)	GAS MARK
Very slow	120	250	½
Slow	150	275-300	1-2
Moderately slow	160	325	3
Moderate	180	350-375	4-5
Moderately hot	200	400	6
Hot	220	425-450	7-8
Very hot	240	475	9

COOKBOOK HOLDERS

Keep your ACP cookbooks clean, tidy and within easy reach with a holder that carries up to 12 books

Photocopy and complete coupon below

Book Holder Australia $13.10 (incl. GST) Elsewhere: $A21.95

Mail or fax Photocopy and complete the coupon below and post to ACP Books Reader Offer, ACP Publishing, GPO Box 4967, Sydney NSW 2001, or fax to (02) 9267 4967.

Phone Have your credit card details ready, then phone 136 116 (within Australia) Mon-Fri, 8.00am-6.00pm; Sat, 8.00am-6.00pm.

Australian residents We accept the credit cards listed on the coupon, money orders and cheques.

Overseas residents We accept the credit cards listed on the coupon, drafts in $A drawn on an Australian bank, and also UK, NZ and US cheques in the currency of the country of issue. Credit card charges are at the exchange rate current at the time of payment.

Mr/Mrs/Ms _____

Address _____

_____ Postcode _____

Country _____ Phone (business hours) _____

Email* (optional) _____

Quantity _____ Total cost $ _____

I enclose my cheque/money order for _____ $ _____

payable to ACP Magazines or please charge _____ $ _____

to my: ☐ Bankcard ☐ Mastercard ☐ Visa ☐ American Express ☐ Diners Club

Expiry date _____

Card number ☐☐☐☐ ☐☐☐☐ ☐☐☐☐ ☐☐☐☐

Cardholder's signature _____

* By including your email address, you consent to receipt of any email regarding this magazine, and other emails which inform you of ACP's other publications, products, services and events, and to promote third party goods and services you may be interested in.
Please allow up to 30 days delivery within Australia. Allow up to 6 weeks for overseas delivery.
Offer expires 31/12/07 HLG06